Don't Be A Spin Sucker

Don't Be A Spin Sucker

What You Need To Know To Restore The Republic Our Founding Fathers Envisioned

George E. Snyder

Writers Club Press
San Jose New York Lincoln Shanghai

Don't Be A Spin Sucker
What You Need To Know To Restore The Republic Our
Founding Fathers Envisioned

Writers Club Press
an imprint of iUniverse.com, Inc.

For information address:
iUniverse.com, Inc.
620 North 48th Street, Suite 201
Lincoln, NE 68504-3467
www.iuniverse.com

ISBN: 0-595-14529-9

Printed in the United States of America

Each day you're being outsmarted and manipulated—and most of the time you don't even know it's happening. This book will open your eyes, show you what to look for, and tell you what you can do about it.

CONTENTS

To My Wife
Karen

INTRODUCTION

Spinners, often referred to as **Spinmeisters** or **Spin Doctors**, surround you. They are so prevalent in your daily life they are continually dumping on you and most of the time you don't even know it. You are just so busy doing what you need to do in your personal life, that **spin seeds** are subconsciously planted within you.

The purpose of this book is to put in perspective the **spin effect** and how it relates to you. While there is **business spin** when it comes to attracting you to products and services, the main emphasis of this book is the daily news and **political spin** consequence.

The information to follow is very direct. Recognizing your personal time is limited and valuable—the author concisely, chapter by chapter, brings to the surface the players and the games that are being played. So that you will be able to get a handle on knowing when you are being **set-up for the spin** you will become

* Familiar with the power of perception
* Knowledgeable about the media effect
* Aware of the serious impact of money
* More informed about the people who run for public office, particularly, lawmakers and what determines how they vote

* Acquainted with the three kinds of lobbyists

closer to the political scene. The information will permit you to better participate in our democracy. Since most of us work five months a year to support the cost of government it should not be just a concern but a responsibility that you know as much as you can about the political process. *After all it is your single largest dollar outlay.*

PRELUDE

Who is this guy who wrote this book? What are his credentials? Where do you think he is coming from? I wonder if he is a liberal or conservative or is it about being a Democrat or Republican? Permit me to put matters in perspective.

I'm a former state senator from Maryland who won four primary and four general elections. Being away from the active political scene for nearly two decades I have had plenty of time to reflect on the public service experience. What made me surface again, and thus this book, is the *political crap* I see going on around us and in my frustrations I just had to sound off and share my experiences and knowledge.

Specific concerns, which this book addresses, are the facts that:

- The citizens of the United States are constantly being used as bait or suckers to politicians' intent on misleading us with the heavy handed use of **spin techniques**.
- Far too many people fluff off the political scene as *politics as usual* and *both sides are just as bad.*
- Thousands of our young people are not getting involved in our political system and they are very much needed.
- Lying, deceit and manipulation are the order of the day.

- With low voter turn outs it is the minority of our electorate that is determining the election results and who becomes our leaders.
- Not enough people have discovered and appreciate that service to others is the best work of life.

I am from a middle class family of four, two boys and two girls. Our dad

after completing business college, became an employee in the office of the Clerk of Circuit Court and later "Clerk", serving until his death. He really didn't like politics but since his position didn't have civil or merit service protection he was subjected to the fear that every four years at election time he could lose his job.

I recall an incident in my life at age 12 when the local Democratic political bosses threatened my father that he would lose his appointive deputy clerk position at the courthouse unless he would accept the party's nomination to run for the office of Registrar of Wills. Dad loved his job in the Clerk's Office which he had held at that time for twenty years. Furthermore, he kept saying the Republican who held the Registrar of Wills position was his close friend and had served in that office for nearly three decades. Dad just didn't want to run. Fear got the best of him and he gave in and filed for the Register of Wills. He hoped he would lose the election and he did by a close margin. During the campaign he would keep out of sight. His only election tool was a single one-face card.

For years the pressure of that incident never left me and my inner conscious kept saying, *George, you got to take on those self-designated political bosses.* When I finished my senior year in college at age 21 I thought I would *take a shot* at trying to be elected to the House of the Maryland Legislature. There were thirteen candidates in the primary election seeking six nominations. I came in fourth at the September primary. At the November general election (the last time paper ballots were used in Maryland), it was announced that I was one of the six elected. I even received the official notice to come to Annapolis, the State Capital, for orientation. Three weeks later, when the official count was formally announced, the Election Board said there was a miscount in the Indian Springs district and I was in the number seven spot and lost.

Needless to say, I was quite upset. What concerned me the most was that I was informed I was defeated by 300 votes in a district where only 170 people voted. I didn't have the money to pay for a recount, which was my expense if the official tally was held correct. With the paper ballot mistake and other suspicions, I was forced to mark up the election as an experience and accept the defeat. I was eager to serve and I saw my election as a vehicle that hopefully could give me some clout to deal with the heavy handed local political boss tactics that existed for years.

A couple of years later I became a Jaycee, a local president, then Maryland State President and from there U.S. Jaycee National Membership Chairman. It was those few years that truly convinced me that service to others is the greatest work of life. At age 29 I made the decision to try politics again and ran for the State Senate and was elected after being vigorously opposed by more than one political boss plus the opposing party. My first term led me to a second term victory. My personal desire was not to serve beyond 8 years, but as I moved up in seniority a third term permitted me to become part of the Senate leadership resulting in a fourth term, whereby I became Senate Majority Leader and Chairman of the Finance Committee.

Choosing not to run again for the state senate, I did contemplate a likely run for governor and even started the campaign. After some reflection I felt I got caught up in all the media attention in my potential candidacy. I just could not stomach the money in the system. In time money led to the downfall and later indictment and conviction of the Governor who ended up serving time in the federal penitentiary.

I have been an entrepreneur since age 13. In order to financially support serving in public office, it has been necessary to continue a career as a marketing consultant. After a couple of years out of the Senate I spent around four years traveling the United States testifying before forty state legislatures, U.S. House and U.S. Senate committees as National Director of the Committee for a Constitutional Amendment for a Balanced Federal Budget. I also served as President of the National Taxpayer's Union (the voice of the American Taxpayer) for a couple of years and have been on its board for over twenty years.

In 1982, I changed from a Democrat to a Republican and ran for the United States Senate from Florida. A great experience, a good run, but I lost. As a former Democrat, who was also a delegate to the forever remembered 1969 Democratic Convention in Chicago, changing parties was not an easy decision to make. But like so many others, I kept witnessing how the Democratic Party was being taken over by several powerful special interest groups and I felt its vast public appeal was being sacrificed. I was motivated by President Ronald Reagan and understood the ground work he was laying for our country's future, which made the change easier.

I am a moderate on social issues and a conservative on fiscal matters. My public service record will also reflect that position. It is a time in my life I sincerely want to "give back and share". I bring to the table what I call 13 + 4 + 16 = 33 year continuing education background referring to K through 12, then 4 years of college, plus 16 years of practical education and *learning as a legislator*. It is my fervent hope you will be enlightened by what you read. I also hope that some of the shared experiences you can put to good use as a responsible citizen in a democratic system.

CHAPTER ONE

ARE THERE JUST THREE BRANCHES OF GOVERNMENT?

The answer is yes, but yet, no. The United States Constitution provides for three: Executive, Legislative, and Judicial. In practice, however, there are five branches.

With the tremendous influence of lobbying, lobbyists through the years have become the non-constitutional fourth branch of government. Sometimes lobbying is referred to as the third tier of Congress and state legislatures. As our country's population increased, and as the democratic system experienced matured lobbying, its related activities became more and more prevalent. As we will discuss lobbying can be a good thing—but it is the extension and reach-out of the lobbying function that is taking away vested rights of our citizens—and putting such into special and privileged hands that have selfish interests. If you were asked the question: Who is the largest employer in Washington, D.C.? Your likely answer would be the federal government. That answer would be wrong. Lobbyists, lawyers, public relations and related personnel engage more people than those who work for the federal government in our Nations Capital.

The fifth branch is the media, which includes print and electronic with television becoming exceptionally powerful. As TV grew through the years the fifteen second sound and picture bites have become very influential. They can make or break an issue or a political career. In politics twenty-four hours can become a life-time.

Yes, there are three constitutional branches but in reality there are five. Media and lobbying can be referred to as the influence branches.

Constitutional Branches	**Influence Branches**
Executive	**Media**
Legislative	**Lobbying**
Judicial	

If you were asked to pick the most powerful branch what would it likely be? Hands down the power of the media would be number one. As we see the expansion of cable and satellite television, along with computer technology, the media power increases. Traditional network audiences are decreasing, but the number of media services and channels are increasing. There are so many television stations, with their own satellite dishes, that often more media people are present covering an event than there are persons attending the affair. At times it is like the media stirring up the event and then reporting about it.

The Judicial branch makes decisions. Virtually all cases have opposing views and seldom is everyone happy with the court's decision. When it comes to filling court vacancies, and most particularly, appointments to the United States Supreme Court, politicians and issue advocates become extremely concerned as to whether the nominee is liberal or conservative.

The Executive and Legislative branches constantly play to the media. It is an inter-active game going on every day.

The Executive branch using its **spin power** to influence the media, and the media pressed to meet daily news deadlines—suspiciously searching for an eye and ear catching headline—thus, the cat and mouse game is always in play. With 535 members of Congress—435 in the House and 100 Senators—each with their own agenda, the media can actually determine the success or failure of the elected office holder. Projecting the proper image on television has particularly become critical.

On the other hand, lobbyists so often want to do everything they can to avoid the media...for the most part a stupid strategy. The hide and seek game can put lobbyists in "back to the wall" situations. Again, the media with the power of exposure comes out the winner.

Therefore, the three constitutional branches in fact have to co-exist with the two influence branches. All five branches are part of the process and each have their own decisive impact on our lives.

Chapter Two

It's Your Nickel

Please, let's get it straight. **The cost of government will cost you and your family more this year than food, clothing, your house mortgage and transportation expenses combined.** Just think how many months you need to work to pay its cost. To not be concerned is worse than ridiculous. To pass off this required dollar outlay with "it is beyond me" is dead wrong.

Again, just think of it—more cost than your mortgage, food and gasoline combined. If you don't show concern you are both foolish and irresponsible for not opening your eyes and recognizing what is really taking place. You're foolish because you are letting it happen with the excuse *there is nothing I can do*. You're irresponsible because you are not participating in and exercising the freedom that so many have died for in order to make your life in a democracy worthwhile. Above all, you are letting your children and grandchildren down. Your non-participation, your lack of concern, and your passing the buck, is already saddling the unborn with huge debt and obligations. It is indeed not a pretty picture.

Add to your own personal expenses the cost of medical insurance, and for numerous families, child care, and you realize that so often there is just the exchanging and recycling of dollars that is taking place. It is not my intent to be a doomsayer, but hopefully to get you to be aware of what is happening around you. And yes, your voice can be heard.

Your share of the tax bite should be sensible and not burdensome. Your nickel has become a lot of nickels. You feel at times you are caught in a vise or you are in the arms of an octopus. Even the elected office holder so often feels the same way in his or her struggle to assist constituents in solving problems. It's not easy. So many things have gotten so involved. The "kiss formula" of keeping things simple, has long ago been tossed out the window when it comes to being a part of or dealing with government. Unfortunately, the "involvement factor" exists at all levels: local, state and federal. The closer you are to the government base and the smaller the local government the better chance you have to have your voice heard.

In spite of the complexity you can make a difference. We must appreciate the government services that are so important to our lives (i.e., good roads, police and fire protection, good education for our children, health protection, etc.). There are far too many people who are single issue oriented. With an attitude of not settling for anything less, their tunnel vision does not permit them to appreciate the importance of other issues and needs.

We likewise must resist temptations to *get my piece of the pie* or that *government owes me* attitudes. It reminds me of the first open public meeting I held shortly after being elected to the State Senate. A gentleman requested a new road, complained about the state park system needing vast improvements and said it was most important we have a new school. He then closed his pitch with, "Senator, keep our taxes down."

CHAPTER THREE

THE PERCEPTION GAME

Perception shows up so often in things we read and hear, and has become so strong in our lives, that more often than not it has become reality. So much of what takes place in your daily life is what others perceive.

With almost everything you do and say, whether in person, by telephone, e-mail or fax, perception is present. We get so wrapped up in our own busy world we don't even think about how we are perceived and forget that others are forming opinions and reacting to us by what they perceive.

All of us want to be liked and most of us have an inner quality and feeling that equates to how others perceive us. What happens, however, is we so often do not recognize the dynamic power of perception as we move about in our daily lives. That same perceptional power reaches beyond individuals, and is so prevalent in television and radio communicating. When it comes to buying products or when a politician is expounding a position on a given issue, perception is in play.

When we do think of perception, there is the usual tendency to believe you are being manipulated or that someone is less than honest in what they are trying to convey. There is no question perception can be abusive. However, certain perceptions can be put to good use. The important factor is to be able to distinguish between perception *to use* and perception *to shun*.

As you look at the description of each kind, mentally visualize or recall situations, incidents, or people who fit the respective categories. By doing so you will be able to quickly identify future perceptions. Consequently, by being more aware of the varying types of perception you can avoid being *duped.* The ten different kinds of Perception are:

<u>TO USE</u>
Conscious
Unconscious
Intellectual
Empowering
Disarming

<u>TO SHUN</u>
Artificial
Calculating
Deceitful
Manipulative
Superficial

PERCEPTIONS TO USE

Conscious: The easiest way to explain conscious perception is that which you are aware and affirmatively set forth in your planning, actions, etc. Examples would be as simple as a person making a good first impression, as in a job interview, a presentation to others or a candidate for public office seeking your vote. Conscious perception is also the way one reacts to varying situations with a knowledge that your actions will create a certain *on-the-spot* image. This type of perception also lends itself to quick adjustments based upon changed circumstances. The conscious perception of a politician is quickly noticed by a watchful potential voter.

Unconscious: This kind of perception emanates from essentially the subconscious. Often times, people have a vision of how they perceive themselves as coming across, but do not reduce that to any affirmative act—they keep it in the back of their mind, so to speak, and evolve the conscious aspect over time. The more deeply developed unconscious kind of perception is what actually kicks into gear and becomes the conscious and visible perception. Successful politicians are cognizant of particular surroundings in their midst as they move about campaigning.

Intellectual: This perception is one that conveys an impression of control and respect. Anyone can, within their abilities, transmit intellectual perception. Everyone has the ability to be good at some or many things. Intellectual perception is not just a function of education or work experience, but rather knowing how to give those receiving the information comfort and security. Making you feel good—and hopefully building comfort and trust between you, the voter, and the person who is seeking public office—can become quite powerful. As this comes about a defined **spin** can seal the positive relationship.

Empowering: This type of perception is one which allows you to build momentum and leverage from positive perceptions. An easy example of empowering is the way you come across to others whether it be friendly, knowledgeable, a person worthy of respect, etc. You can in a one-on-one situation, within a group, convert what could be a sluggish conversation into a more energetic and positive interplay. By kicking up your actions, you are empowered to take the lead. Therefore, you can reshape mold or direct.

Disarming: A perception that is disarming is one that is as easy as a smile. Do you ever wonder why politicians love being photographed holding a baby? Such is positive and generates happiness and good feelings. Disarming perception can be asserted in situations where you convey comments that essentially call the other person's bluff and will get things back on the proper track.

PERCEPTIONS TO SHUN

Artificial: When one hears about the power of perception, artificial usually comes to mind. We are in a world congested with fake or short-term thoughts, in which the standard becomes *the end justifies the means*. Artificial perception can be manufactured information and thoughts. They are promises that will never be kept, which are as simple as, *I will get back to you later, let me handle it from here*, etc. A person who says things without any regard as to follow-through, truthfulness, or accountability, is an artificial predator. Like a politician saying, *we've got to fix this problem*, and then does nothing when it comes to working on the solution.

Calculating: The easiest way to equate this kind of perception is by identifying the manipulator. The **spin doctors** that have received all the publicity in politics bring this one to the forefront. Calculating can be positive in the development of a programmed image and plan, but also can be very negative if its motives are insincere, dishonest, and lack concern for the impact on others.

Deceitful: Is really a combination of artificial, calculating, manipulative, and superficial perceptions. Acts which are downright untrue or dishonest, and are done to mislead, makeup the highest and most dangerous kinds of negative perception. This type of perception is unwarranted in any scenario and is without justification.

Manipulative: Has a personality that can be positive or negative. Many individuals feel they are being manipulated by even going through the process of orchestrating, planning, or developing a plan to create a certain perception. It is not manipulative if it is done with sincerity, a sensitivity to its impact, and doesn't go outside the boundaries of honesty and integrity. The negative side of manipulative perception is that which causes one to adapt and alter their thoughts to *get their way*. These efforts, if discerned by others, can lead to a lack of trust and confidence, and a loss of future credibility.

Superficial: This kind of perception is essentially the physical or outward displays that seem to captivate others, but are either without substance or foundation. Superficial can be the person who says, *nice to see you*, when they can't stand you. Superficial perception exists throughout our world particularly in this age of electronic media. Interpersonal relationships have become less important, and the fast pace of life and lack of loyalty, allows people to get away with short-term words to just cover the moment.

Because *Perception* is powerful—even to the point that much of the time its power overcomes reality and in doing so, the *Perception* becomes the reality. By being aware of the different kinds of perceptions you will be able to see through **cons** and **spins** and react accordingly.

CHAPTER FOUR

FUNDRAISERS, MEDIA CONSULTANTS & POLL TAKERS

There is no question that political campaigns require money. There isn't anything wrong with a candidate for public office putting in place a fund raising capability. The issue, however, becomes how much money to raise and more importantly from what sources. With numerous candidates having media consultants, who in turn want pollsters involved, the *handlers* can take a good candidate and make him or her into something they are not. Thus, a masquerade or phony candidate.

The orchestration creates a sham at the outset. The focus is solely on winning and for so many Election Day winners there are years of pressure, feeling *locked in* and being downright uncomfortable. Their candidacies were **spun** to get the votes. The **spinning** regarding many positions on issues are not the true feelings of the office holder.

What happens is the political managers know their success depends on how much money is raised and at the same time they work with the other *handlers* to avoid taking unpopular positions on vulnerable issues. The lack of sincerity then needs to be camouflaged with the **spin**. The *true inner being* of the elected official remains captive and in effect he or she is acting the role.

Sell-outs can begin early on when a specific special interest/issue group brings pressure to bear on the candidate. The candidate is rightfully interviewed by the respective groups on positions and issues that concern them. What they are seeking is a commitment from the candidate regarding specific legislations. When they hear things they like then comes the money. Money can be *in-kind help*, contributions or both. The game is to get the candidate committed even before he is elected. Labor and teacher unions use such tactics to the fullest extent. The combination of people and money can be quite strong.

As the fundraiser (F) is looking for campaign funds he targets specific special interest audiences. The media handler (M) sees an opening for his candidate to *make news* but first wants the re-enforcement of the campaign's poll taker (P). The results of that process lead to the candidate saying and doing things that others want to hear so he can get more money and hopefully more votes. Usually there's little consideration given to how the candidate sincerely feels about the issue. The process, which generally is *something I can live with* rationalization perpetuates a dissimulation. Therefore, F + M + P = Deceitful Candidate.

We read and hear about so many candidates moving to the center or to the left or to the right. With their insincerity they are positioning themselves to please a certain pressure group(s), because their pollsters tell them this is what they need to do, to *get through the primary election* but *then we can worry about moving over to a different position in the general election.* Little consideration is given to what the candidate's position is with regard to what is the best interest of the general public and even what the candidate feels is right. Here again *just tell them what they want to hear* so we can tap the money source. This technique is used frequently by candidates who are labeled too extreme, as too liberal or too conservative—to jockey to a centrist stand just to get through the election. Then their pitch is *I discovered new information* which now requires them to alter their position. With all this the **con** worked and the voters become **spin-suckers**.

Hillary Clinton, the President's wife is a known far to the left liberal. In her ambitious need and pursuit of power to win a U.S. Senate seat from New York she is projecting herself as a moderate. A good example of doing whatever it takes to get votes. Her focus is on winning the office for herself. Yes, placing self ahead of her beliefs and later dealing with things that relate to representing the people. Usually Democrats run liberal in the primary elections as Republicans run conservative and then in order to get elected, the presidential candidates, in particular, will move to the center in the general election in the hope of reaching the swing vote of independent thinking voters.

For over twenty years Republican Party leaders have encouraged *open primaries.* That is encouraging Independent and Democrats to vote in their primaries with the hope some newcomers would stick with their party in the general election. A real case can be made that *closed primaries* only permit party members to vote. In those situations independent voters really become dependent on the respective political party primary election decisions.

The Vice President Al Gore versus Bill Bradley contest for the Democratic presidential nomination brought to the forefront some very strong historical differences in the candidates. That is Gore's career of many years serving in both houses of the Congress and Bradley's three terms in the U.S. Senate. Gore has a history of changing votes on significant issues as he does makeovers of himself both in his appearance and campaign style. The former New Jersey senator also had his eighteen year record to defend. Many of Bradley's heavy punches were left over for the Republicans to use against Gore in the General Election.

In politics votes cast twenty years ago are on the table. Consultants to candidates look for *hooks* so they can exploit media attention that hopefully will reach the voter. It may be a vote at the time which was really not that significant but is now a natural to use for the **spin**. Making a mountain out of a molehill and taking things out of context can get quite nasty. With this comes the **con**.

I have played a role or have been a participant in numerous political campaigns over a lot of years, but the South Carolina Republican Primary 2000 was about the sneakiest, nastiest, and most intense campaign for the presidential nomination one could witness. The Republican Party hierarchy decided a couple years before that they were going to determine who is going to be the Republican nominee. Using a method of taking a brand name, raising lots of money for the candidate (around 70 million dollars as a starter), and in effect intimidating other candidates they would hopefully lock up the party nomination. Governor George W. Bush of Texas, the former President's son was their choice. Although the younger Bush only had six years of public office service— the **spin** has been to project him as the successful Governor of the second largest state in the nation— and boast of his great executive capabilities. In spite of this effort around a dozen other Republican hopefuls announced their candidacy and in turn spent lots of time and money campaigning. For most, around a year later they withdrew from the race prior to the first primary in New Hampshire. That election narrowed the field to three candidates, with two front runners.

U.S. Senator John McCain of Arizona, a maverick, war hero, and populist candidate, pulled an upset in New Hampshire defeating Governor Bush by nineteen percentage points. With less than three weeks to go to the South Carolina primary Bush and the Republican establishment was faced with a must win in South Carolina. Being in nearby North Carolina during this time I could see from the media spill-over what was taking place. With the exception of two Congressmen the South Carolina Republican political musclemen supported Bush. Millions upon millions of dollars were spent. With the Republican bosses working in concert with the Christian Right Movement Bush won over McCain by eleven percentage points.

Every conceivable communication capability was put to use in this campaign both in the air and on the ground. It was impossible to escape the election, for whenever televisions and radios were turned on, there was a saturation of campaign advertising. Tons of mailings, faxes, e-mails, signs everywhere and constant telephoning. Many of these *below the radar* tactics were *worse than terrible*. For example, using *push polling*, which is third party phone call bashing of one's opponent. This technique allows candidates to smear their adversaries without getting their own hands dirty. Nasty misinformation and lies all over the place. Counting the dollars spent by issue advocates,

Bush outspent McCain eight to one and with all this the 70 million dollar Bush Campaign funds were down to 20 million dollars.

The amazing feat of this experience is that it clearly shows that negative advertising works and that the **spin-meisters** in a couple weeks with the use of money and propaganda can bombard an electorate. It was a game of mimic and attack. McCain was the "reformer" in New Hampshire. Bush dropped his campaign theme *compassionate conservative* and pitched and displayed everywhere that he was the *reformer with results*. Bush ran a TV attack advertisement against McCain. McCain answered with a negative television advertisement that was over zealous and had a reference comparing Bush to President Clinton. Bush blasts McCain for going over the line. McCain says he will not run any more negative television advertising. Bush increases his negative advertising attacks on McCain.

McCain used his campaign bus to travel everywhere he went in a given state. It particularly received much media attention in the New Hampshire campaign. He invited reporters to ride with him. Normally the large number of media people would follow candidates in a companion bus. By being accessible to the media McCain in effect had an on going press conference that would last from early morning to late at night. Bush was more guarded and used scheduled press coverage and structured audiences to deliver his message as McCain held open town hall meetings.

People say they don't like negative TV advertisements but election results and particularly in the Bush versus McCain South Carolina contest, shows they work. The thirty second sound bite registered with many voters because, by having so many advertisements on TV and radio, there is a subconscious connection. Most people are busy with their daily living and they do not look beyond the **spin**. Generally, negative advertising by a candidate also forces his opponent to respond as McCain did to Bush's first attack.

What is also wild about all this is where the media conducted *exit polls*, the electorate felt that Bush was a bigger reformer than McCain. The voters also felt that McCain ran more negative advertising than Bush when in actuality it was the reverse. By imitating, teaming with an issue advocate constituency, having most of the party political operatives on deck, and lots of money, Bush won. The **spin** worked **big time**.

Chapter Five

Spin Doctors Surround You

The **spin doctors** and **spinmeisters** surround us. Because so many people just don't care it is absolutely amazing what they get away with at your expense. The **spin** is not just in the political arena, which is by far more prevalent, but also takes place in business.

Public relations and advertising are great services and we all need to be informed. We have come a long way in being conscious of truth in packaging and identifying the plus and minus of consumer products we purchase, whether they be food or drugs. Information is critical to our very existence. Accredited information also becomes knowledge we can use. Naturally, whoever is conveying the message is going to put the best face on it. There certainly is nothing wrong with showing the favorable side of any situation.

The threat is the outright lies and deceit. Witness the games being played surrounding the tobacco industry while people die from the harm the products bring to the population. The manipulation going on in the national political arena is just passed off by so many as politics as usual. Even worse is the outright ignoring of the issues by always placing self as number one and letting the rest of the world go by.

Tobacco interests are restricted as to television advertising and certain related advertising methods. They claim they will be able to cut back the growing number of teenagers starting to use tobacco. This for the most part is nothing but lip service. The industry constantly finds ways through music, sports events, wearing apparel, and movies, to still get across its message. **Spinners** are constantly looking for openings all the time and in effect are making smoking cool. When the message gets through that it is not cool to smoke, then, and most likely only then, will tobacco usage drop. **Spinners'** time should be focused on this issue and it would seem the **spin** has to somehow come to surface through the peer system. A ninth grade Denver, Colorado class did a survey within a couple of miles of their school on the amount of cigarette advertising directed to school children. They were astonished that advertising was everywhere. Some of it quite subtly done and was directed to five year old children. The advertising was also much heavier in Hispanic and African American communities. In their anger, they brought a resolution before the City Council to ban advertising near schools, a hopeful sign that may encourage other children to respond in their areas. *Increasing the price of tobacco through taxation is not going to solve the cool* problem.

Through lack of awareness action, life for many just goes on with the attitude the problem is always with the other person and will never hit me. Here is an industry that has consistently lied to us and obviously will continue to do so as long as it can. As the issue became hotter in the United States the cigarette lobby continues to use misconception techniques in other parts of the world so as to maintain market share. Money, not lives, is their interest. Extremely cruel.

Look at the numerous TV commercials you view in the three to four minute commercial breaks taken during television programming. In a prime time, one hour program, one-fourth of the time is directed to advertising. You'll notice many advertisements spend more time on making you feel good, than on the product itself. Also, the care given to consumer product packaging is critical in obtaining consumer acceptances. These perceptions and their **spins** can mean the difference between success and failure of many products. As long as the influence elements are forthright and honest—good can come from the **spin**. **It is the outright lying schemes to defraud us; attempts to insult our individual intelligence; and the manipulation of the facts, that need to be our concern.**

Spin doctors and **Spinmeisters** have been gradually increasing their power of influence through the years. With the growth of television and the importance of the media in getting the consumer's attention and arousing the voter, more and more people, under numerous disguised professional titles, are working in this field. With the wide use of polls and surveys we hear on a daily basis what is supposedly happening around us. For the television and radio industries, it is about ratings—which means dollars. For products and services, it is the market size increase and share—which mean dollars. For the person running for office, it means—the more dollars spent, the more likelihood of more votes. With all this, the million dollar production cost for preparing the TV commercial and the need for people seeking public office to be substantially wealthy or to virtually spend the majority of their time raising money is insane. With money always in the lead so many worthy people and worthwhile concerns fade into the sunset.

In politics the modern practice of using **spin tactics** has become common. There is no question the highest office in the United States has become a *media presidency*. I believe if Thomas Jefferson and Abraham Lincoln were to run for president today they would have a difficult time getting elected and our country would have lost two thoughtful and dynamic leaders. Jefferson was a weak public speaker and the "Lincoln look" certainly would not have been TV compatible.

History reveals we want our Presidents to be good communicators. Sincerity coupled with a charismatic style motivates and is impressive to the electorate. For example, Presidents Franklin Roosevelt, John Kennedy and Ronald Reagan all had effective charms and persuasive powers. They used their attributes to lead. Each handled difficult and controversial situations while using the best face possible in communicating with the American people. To go beyond and intentionally focus on the **spin of the day**, respond to the polls to keep ratings high, and not be forthright with the American people, is not only unfair but wrong.

Just think about it. The President's press secretary and staff not only attempt to manage the news—but they package it in the way that the polls tell them to do—in their quest for broad base appeal...like an on going political campaign *that we need to win*. In the **spin** process they embark upon the misleading gray area that can so easily lead to outright mistruths. As taxpayers we are paying sizeable salaries to high level White House employees who spend half or more of their time **spinning us**. They also devote considerable energy to plotting media strategy which includes when and where to *break the story*. Like a football game, they watch how it is being received by the media and chalk up the score. In Chapter Seven, **spin techniques** used by the Clinton administration are detailed.

Mean spirited **professional spinners** like James Carville, the President's buddy, regularly plan **spins** using artificial, calculating, deceitful, manipulative, and superficial perceptions—all five perceptions that need to be watched. The **spin** is to confuse us, create doubt, always involve the other guy, and place the blame on someone else. It's downright dishonest and extremely manipulative and it should not be that way. The individual intelligence of the American people has been insulted.

Because many of us want to look the other way, we fall for the **continuous spins** on a regular basis. Our individual selfishness says, I'm doing okay and it is best if I just let it be—it really doesn't matter. It *does* matter. The democratic system of governing are at stake. The respect our children have for our democracy is at stake. Our morals and the ten commandments are at stake. America's credibility and place in the world is at stake. Yes, it matters and the only thing that counts, is *the good economy*, is very short-sighted. Corruption and deceit undermines each of our lives and our civic responsibility.

Guys like Carville are out to discredit their targets at any cost. Gangsters have hot-shot men and heavy-handed politicians have their **spinmeisters**. There isn't an ounce of sincerity in what they do. They just have to attack, attack and attack. Their philosophy is to perpetuate an untruth and repeat and repeat it often enough that listeners will believe it is the truth. They also live with *we'll get even* attitudes. Serious and concerned citizens can readily identify their **spins** and check them off as loud mouths and noise makers. Unfortunately, not enough people pay attention.

The use of *smoke and mirrors* has been around from day one. However, so often the public *gets set up* **big time** and generally with our own taxpayer dollars. For example, a politician taking an issue he is really against and making out that he is for it because of *special interest* pressure. In the process he purposely provokes a fight over the matter—only to then *blame it on others* that the matter failed. Another insincere move is when a lawmaker gets another legislator to sponsor a bill he knows will attract opposition—and he opposes the measure knowing *his position* will likely gain him political support and future campaign contributions. Real bad stuff. Such is the equivalent of your setting fire to your house and standing outside as it burns seeking and accepting sympathy. Particularly during elections, candidates from opposing sides relish pulling copy out of context and using it to their advantage. Not only is the idea to distract—but to produce a few second damaging sound bite **spin**. When anyone anywhere feels shafted, misled or victimized, more people need to talk about it.

In a democracy you have every right to speak out. The Carville types sure do. Of course, much of it is for show and to make money. Many lives can be affected from what they *stir-up* and where we differ we must blast back. The fodder they dump on us has a terrible smell and it needs to be deodorized and often pitched back in their faces. Crap is rubbish and it needs to be treated accordingly.

Chapter Six

Media & Pundit Effect

We complain about the media but we should also ask ourselves "what do you think politics would be like without them." Unequivocally the answer would be the bad guys would get away with taking everything they could get their hands on short of the dome of the Capitol. As we will discuss in Chapter Ten the great percentage of elected officials are honest, respectful, and decent people. As in business and the professions there is a small percentage of bad apples in every bushel. Most likely the percentage of uncouth elected officials may be less than other professions and fields of endeavor primarily because of the watchful eyes of the media.

In better understanding the media it becomes necessary to divide the press (print) from the electronic media which includes television, radio and the internet. The majority of the people get their news from TV, thus the time-limited coverage and need for the few second *sound and pic bites*. Radio also had time limitations except for *talk radio* which goes into the depth of the news. With radio, the listener *hears better* whereby pic bites can distract the audio. The print media cover the full story in daily newspapers as well as weekly, bi-monthly and monthly magazines. It is questionable how powerful their editorial pages are on reaching out to the masses. Their positions, however, are regularly quoted by other media and when scandal breaks their investigative reporting capabilities perform a most important public service. For the person seeking public office and his supporters it is a great feeling to receive newspaper endorsements, particularly in print where they have reproductive value.

With national television networks doubling from the traditional big three, and with the significant growth of cable channels, the media market exposure has become fragmented. What has occurred on television are in-depth programs that allocate time to issues of the day and particularly to major political campaigns. Nightly hour shows like "Hardball with Chris Matthews" and the "Hannity & Colmes" are performing valuable service to the electorate. Fairness practices give the viewer an opportunity to hear both sides. Their audiences are increasing and the programs can become addictive to the viewer.

Hardball's televised college tour during the 2000 presidential campaign has been impressive and certainly is stimulating and hopefully will encourage younger voters to get involved in the political process. Pundits (persons who make comments or judgments) make up most of the guests. These are the programs to see and hear where the **masters of spin** show their true colors. Like sporting events they become combative and that is good. Many pundits work for major publications and are featured columnists. More and more shows are engaging different view political consultants.

Radio programs such as Rush Limbaugh, ably go into the depth of selected news stories and explore issues and public officials beyond what the core press is reporting. Rush lets you know exactly where he stands and you clearly know as a listener you are listening to the conservative view. The Sunday morning news programs (i.e., Meet The Press, This Week, Face The Nation, News Sunday, etc.) offer in depth reporting as well as news analysis.

The explosion that has taken place with all kinds of media growth—and then add satellite dishes, helicopters and other news technology—the media can often have more people present to cover a candidate or an event than the number of people in the audience. Every media person present needs to file his or her story. There is a lot of *got-cha* play taking place. Obviously, they get in each others way and there will always be tensions between print and the electronic media. Also think of the involvement that surrounds the President of the United States in that there are two thousand authorized White House correspondents.

Candidates for public office who shy away from the media only damage themselves. A democracy is an open government and that is why we have sunshine laws to make certain the public interest and the public funding of matters are not dealt with secretly. Unfortunately, for many politicians their handlers want the candidates best side to always show and with it they want a controlled environment. The media can be tough. They, like any of us, can make human mistakes. *If you feel you have been wronged* by a particular media person there certainly will always be enough other media folks around to listen to your view. Of course, whatever it is must be newsworthy. Some politicians like making the media *a scapegoat.* Making the media the *whipping boy* is a dangerous and risky way to go. The real power is within their control. For their outreach is in place and it never stops. Of course, whenever anyone feels they are right, whatever that call may be, they should certainly speak out and clearly express their view. That is what democracy is all about.

Public officials and candidates for elected offices need to be *very open*. They are serving, for a specific period of time, the general public and should not be in the pockets of special interest groups. Politicians are always on center stage and whatever they do in their life, both public and private, becomes *open season*. If they can't deal with it they are likely in the wrong profession.

CHAPTER SEVEN

BEING THE BEST BUT YET THE WORST ALL IN ONE

The title of this chapter specifically refers to William Jefferson Clinton, the two term elected President of the United States. Without question, nearly everyone is tired of the *Clinton Matter*. As much as we like it to go away it never will. The man worries about his legacy but that die has already been cast in that he is the first *elected* U.S. President to have ever been impeached. That is what history has already recorded. A book dealing with being **conned, spun and re-spun** would not be complete without including the **spin techniques** of the Clinton administration.

In the early 1990's what appeared as a fresh, intelligent, attractive and viable candidate for the highest office has unveiled a man who from the very beginning of his run for the presidency, decided to play the game of misconception. He was elected on a lie. His desire then and throughout his presidency is to do whatever it takes to win. Position issues, people and situations—polls will show what the public wants to hear. It's not about leadership and solving problems but what can he do to keep winning and be popular. It's me first with the affairs of the country tagged on second and third along the perceptions path. Through masterful and deceitful manipulation Clinton and his cronies have done extremely well in getting their **spin** into the minds of a large percentage of the electorate. The offensive techniques that *both sides do it* and *it's nothing but politics as usual* kept his ratings high. Sadly, the more the **spinners** get away with *things* the more it erodes the electorate sense of responsibility to be effective citizens.

Unfortunately, most Americans can no longer distinguish between fact and what has been manufactured as fact. The old political cliché that when things are economically good *people vote their pocketbook* certainly has been an advantage for Clinton. If the economy would have dropped Clinton would *have been gone.*

Perception can always outplay complacency. The **spinners** know that and milk it for all it's worth. Few of us take time to recognize that the good economy of the last decade of the century started with economic policies prior to Clinton taking office. The impact of computer technology from American inventors and entrepreneurs has so positively and dramatically affected our economy and the United State's position in the world. Regardless of who is holding the office of President, most of what surrounds us would have still come to fruition. The sitting President has every right to claim the success and it is good politics to do so. However, to take the front and perpetuate it as a way to hide corruption, lying, deceit and wrong, is not only unfair but is eating away and damaging the very foundation of our democratic existence.

Clinton and his crafty team on a regular basis use eight of the ten perceptions identified in Chapter Three. Five of these perceptions can be treacherous. If anyone has ever walked on the edge in American public life it has been Bill Clinton. To this writer he has not yet come to grip, and likely never will, with the fact that he alone creates his own problems. He lives a life of lies and has always blamed things that go wrong on the other person. He is a man who feels he can charm his way out of any situation. So sad for this *master politician* has **conned** his family, associates and all the people of our great country. His wife, Hillary, in her quest to maintain and enhance her craving for power is like him in that she will also lie and distort the truth. As a candidate for the U.S. Senate she also orchestrates positions guided by the polls.

As you look at the **spin** list to follow, determine whether or not you have been **conned**. Of course, things have been passed off by so many as *politics as usual*. I must say it is still hard to believe that certain respected and deliberate members of the U.S. Senate did not have the courage to deal with the Clinton situation—early on in the best interest of our country—when the U.S. House of Representatives Articles of Impeachment came before the Senate. *Partisan politics* and lack of *guts* prevailed.

The Presidential Spin List:

- The President's press secretary and press office not only packages the news but they also attempt to manage it. Favorite media personnel receive advantages. If it is good news, get it on television as fast as you can. If it is lousy, try to feed it out late Friday, and in print first, where the impact will be less.
- To anyone that attacks us or has said derogatory things, *get them* and destroy them with any kind of

spin that can ruin their credibility so we can at least get on an even playing field.

- Tell the public you want to get it over with real soon and at the same time do all you can to delay. Then use legal issues and the courts to hopefully win the advantage of time. Such tactics are both hypocritical and manipulative and are **cons** directed at the American people.

- Admit little, even though there is much more.

- Find an issue people like, or one you can take from the other side— and just go for it—and naturally take the credit.

- To take attention away from the scandals develop a small news story into a big one.

- Place some of our former consultants and key employees as independent pundit sources so they can regularly defend us on the television circuit and talk shows.

- Do as few press conferences as possible and then team it with a foreign dignitary.

- Plan many trips to other countries and stay as long as you can to keep the public's attention away from other matters. This looks presidential and minimizes things at home. Forget about the cost for after all the American taxpayer will pick up the tab.

- Follow the formula that if the *subject* has appeal keep talking about it. Don't make too many waves, for people will know you're for it. When nothing happens, it is not us, it is the other guy that didn't act who killed it.

- Blame it on the prosecutor (knowing there is little he can say until all investigative facts are in) and make him and his staff the bad guys. Without a doubt this is a most disreputable attack on our democratic system of government.
- When things go wrong, blame it on the media.
- When the media brings up personal problems, say nothing or very little. Just refer the matter to the President's lawyers for they are handling the case.
- As each question surfaces, just answer by side stepping as much as you can.
- Schedule lots of issues for media coverage day in and day out, particularly when Congress is out of session.

And on and on it goes. When Dick Morris, the political advisor to President

Clinton, had his personal shameful problem, the strategy was to just tell the public he's no longer around and then use the telephone to keep in touch. When reckless and relentless fund raising procedures surfaced, *play innocent* and know little about it for you are *busy* with the people's business. Just tell them what they want to hear. In a day of so it will blow away.

The President of the United States should possess the highest morals and characters and be a role model not only for our children, but also for the world. Any corporate executive who committed just a few of the alleged wrongs would have been fired. It's very disheartening to have a newscaster tell us we may not want to have our children watch or hear the next news story, that relates to sensitive matters, originating from the oval office.

There is a substantial difference between a President using his charismatic charm and persuasive capabilities and a President establishing what is in effect a **Department of Spin,** within the White House at the expense of the American taxpayer.

The Presidency has become a spectator sport. With the involvement of money, corruption, and sex, it became not only the new daytime television soap but the prime time TV serial. With exposure on television of so many things regarding crime, sensational events, foul language, etc., to many, the Clinton mess wasn't a big deal. They have looked the other way as the President was obsessed with himself. *Fake concern* for our country's children, morals and family values has not been in the best public interest. I am convinced that if there would be a public office of *World President* Clinton would enjoy running for it. His crafty use of **spin** and his ability to compartmentalize his personal life and issues would make him a front runner. Unfortunately, Clinton did not respect *The Office of the President* as much as many of our concerned citizens.

CHAPTER EIGHT

MONEY, MONEY
& MORE MONEY

There never seems to be enough money. Most candidates for public office are still raising money after the election to cover the deficit. The winners are sworn into office and then the demands from the public and the bureaucracy are pressing them for more and more money for their pet projects. This is—enough money to get elected—and when you win, the demands of public and the bureaucracy keep wanting more and more money. The late U.S. Senator Everett Dicksen said it well, *a million dollars here and a million dollars there and soon we are talking about serious money.* Today billions are tossed around instead of millions.

Money power and campaign financing has been talked about extensively for decades. In fact, in most of my campaigns I made *money and its trade-offs* the issue. In spite of what the reports say money is not the only ingredient necessary to win public office. Of course, it does require money to run. However, a good candidate with a newsworthy message can eliminate the need for a considerable amount of money. How? It is much better to be in the news at no cost than to pay the tremendous expense of television advertising. The media reports the sizeable outlay of dollars for the respective political campaigns. With around three-fourths of most campaign expenditures paying for television and radio commercials—the bulk of the campaign dollars go into the pockets of the media. Those very dollars pay the salaries and expenses of the reporters that so often criticize the money in the system.

The concern is not just how much a candidate spends on his campaign, but where he gets the money and what he has to exchange to get that financial support. The astronomical costs of waging political campaigns and winning elective offices today has pushed the dollar into such a dominant position. Money has become the material which cements most of the relationships in the monopoly game of government and politics. I feel that it is not necessary for so much money to be spent. Such a tremendous outlay seems to be to be a waste and can lead to even more waste of the taxpayer's money when it comes time for certain contributors to be rewarded.

As absurd and staggering to the mind as these costs are, they would not pose a serious threat to the survival of our democratic system of government were it not for the conditions they create. A politician eyeing elective office must face the problem of where to go to secure the inflated sums of money which have become necessary to finance a campaign. This is where the significance of the dollar becomes not only dominant but also dangerous.

Money exchange is *the cesspool of American politics.* Money is the commodity which makes government distant from the people by magnifying the voices of special interests and diluting the voices of the voters. The high costs of campaigning often have served to restrict access to the political arena to those few candidates who are able to secure financial support from the individuals, special interest organizations and businesses who are in a financial position to provide that support. The distinction between a campaign contribution and a bribe are difficult to detect.

When two people contribute two million dollars or so to pay the cost of *last minute negative television advertising*, by setting up a fake disbursement committee, money in the political system has really gone to far. Then for the other candidate, who benefits from the money to say *I didn't know anything about it* is mighty difficult to digest. Maybe he didn't know *on purpose* for to know is illegal. Virtually no one anywhere, in my judgment, is going to spend that much money without a return favor.

Why do most political consultants (remember (F) and (M) in Chapter Four) keep pressing for more and more money? Because they almost always *get a piece of the action* and their mind set is *more money gives us a better chance of winning*. Unfortunately, so often their focus is not just on their candidate's success but is getting *as much as I can* to cover the dry spell until the next election.

If our political system worked democratically, as it was originally intended to function, each individual who desired to serve the public in elective office would have equal access to seeking that office and he or she would derive their campaign support from a broad based proportion of the American population. The way our system functions in reality limits the number of people who are able to seek public office. So often the winners have been supported by a very small percentage of the population—which consisted of powerful blocks of special interest voters. Thus, the decisions made in the halls of government are to accommodate a few. They give politicians the money because the office holder has the power. Through special interest contributions to campaigns these interests come to wield tremendous influence over government officials who become indebted to them. Public servants who should be representative of the entire electorate therefore become obligated to the very few. In essence, they function as little more than *elected lobbyist.*

If too much money comes from a few sources the elected official can become a private rather than a public official. It's most unfortunate that many public servants have accepted the contribution system as a political way of life and therefore were **hooked** before even being elected to public office. Naturally, they are not in a position to freely speak against the system or offer meaningful cures. It is vital that public officials be impartial and independent thinkers, that public office not be used for personal advantage, and that the public have confidence in the integrity of its government. We must press for reform in our method of campaign financing which, in return for contributions of campaign dollars, renders the political official indebted to and controlled by special interests. We must liberate our political officials from the ills, pressures and debts of the present system.

Strong leadership from the Executive and Legislative branches can stop this insane system. Lip service and continual delays work against the public interest. It is not an easy task but a resolution is possible. In solving the problem there needs to be an attack on four fronts: spending levels, individual contributions, enforcement and disclosure. Getting rid of unlimited soft money and cash contributions is a must.

Of course, those who form the *invisible government* which so often is a part of some communities and states, are not wanting to lose the control they have over certain public officials. These *power brokers* operate as unseen agents dispensing the fruits of government without any real claim to the title of power. Really bad. Government in all states of this nation, must cease functioning in a game-like atmosphere of team-member mentality and power monopolies. The power of the people must always be returned to the people through their elected representatives.

I wrote about the need for true campaign financing reform twenty-five years ago. The Richard Nixon scandal and his resignation from the Presidency brought much of the problem to light. Some changes were made only to open the door to more abuse and loop holes as time progressed. Therefore it is easy for one to say *regardless what laws are passed the rascals will figure away to get around them.*

Now let's look a little further in-depth. A President and Congress that seriously want to bring reform to the American taxpayer can and should adopt a tax system that in effect throws out the tax code. Call it flat tax or whatever you like. Our tax return can be as simple as a single sheet of paper. The massive use of computers will even make it more efficient. The formula can take care of low income concerns and we can all be treated fairly. Sure the Internal Revenue Service will need fewer personnel; public accountants won't be as busy; the American citizen will have more productivity and available time; there will be fewer *heart attacks from worry*; and with all this the *big-buck* campaign contributors will not be able to use their money to get treated more favorably by getting *exempt. An aroused public can and will make it happen.*

Never forget that when privileged groups/people *receive favor* the average citizen gets *short changed.*

We must no longer allow an atmosphere which encourages power brokerage, enticed contributions, and chastisement of elected officials who dare to challenge the system that exists within this great country. More of us need to see the **big picture—prioritize—and stop perpetuating our existence.**

A discussion of money in our political system must also include *money and the bureaucracy.* There will never be enough money to please the government bureaucracy. Bureaucrats say to themselves *treat the lawmaker nicely but many of them will come and go and we will still be here.* These unspoken sentiments of many state and federal employees in top merit and civil service positions underlie a basic condition in government which has distorted the legitimate function of the bureaucracy. A bureaucracy in any organization is the established machinery by which the organization operates—the rules, procedures, guidelines, and authority which are necessary for efficient and productive functioning. In government, the bureaucracy is most often connected with the executive branch and the cabinet departments of health, transportation, social services, etc. which remain constant while legislators come and go.

As lobbyists have been designated the *third house* of the legislature, the bureaucracy has often been referred to as the *fourth branch* of government. I did not include them as a *branch of government* in Chapter One. I feel the Congress and State Legislatures have the power to over rule bureaucratic dominance. History clearly shows that, whatever the form of government, bureaucracies are here to stay. With the advent of expanding industry, mass production, scientific developments, and inventions come the need for certain regulations. As professions and occupational fraternities, they encourage the formation of agencies to police activities within a given area. Hence, a bureaucracy grows in a society to meet these needs.

In our modern era it would be impossible to do without the bureaucracy as an institution of government. In a broad sense it plays a most important role in the overall governmental program. As umpire and referee in many areas of our economic, societal, and governmental life, the bureaucracy has permitted orderly furtherance of our basic democratic principles. It renders far reaching and beneficial assistance to the community in terms of maintaining health programs, transportation systems, and economic assistance to the poverty stricken. And, in many cases, it provides legislatures with sorely needed information, advice, and guidance in setting complex government policy.

However, the public's image of the government bureaucrats, their functions and their activities, is often colored with cynicism and suspicion. John Q. Public associates bureaucracy negatively with red tape, unqualified personnel, power craving and self-serving functionaries, and an overindulgence in routine procedures without respect for human relationships. Often these associations are simple bellyaching. On the other hand, there are many times when such comments reflect reality. I think it can safely be said that the bureaucracy itself, mainly through the impressions many of its own participants create, has brought about its own poor public image.

The expansion of bureaucracies on all levels of government has received the most public criticism. This expansion has made the public more suspicious than ever of bureaucrats and many citizens feel that, as such, the bureaucracy is harming our American way of life. The constant abuse of the system by some bureaucrats is doing much to erode public confidence. The public easily suspects the bureaucrat who keeps expanding into areas of service which, though worthwhile, could be more economically handled by other means. Legislators can quickly detect—through experience and the necessity of getting along with people—the bureaucrat who is sincere, hardworking, and dedicated to his or her legitimate mission—as opposed to the one who is a power-craving phony.

There are times when bureaucrats, whose budget requests have been slashed, become so overwhelmed by frustration that they resort to alternatives that range from wondrous to whacky. They build and keep building their public relations capabilities so they can put out their **spin** on an on going basis.

The real trouble with the bureaucracy occurs when it oversteps the legitimate boundaries of its purpose and function. In theory, the purpose of the bureaucracy is to carry out the policies which are set by elected officials. However, the seasoned lawmaker sadly realizes that *it just doesn't work that way* all the time. They play on their influence, power and tactical skills to build *little empires* and to *grab for more power.* These bureaucrats strive not simply to provide the machinery by which policy is executed, but seek to make the policy themselves.

When a bureaucratic leader can find ways within his little empire to shelve some people, add others, change job classifications to suit his desires, make rules and regulations to suit his purposes, build a public relations department tailored to his personal wants, have his own paid lobbyist, stall programs he was directed to inaugurate, play hide and seek on projects for years and years, add new programs without reevaluating old ones, find ways to add more cars and better offices, and be granted a lifetime job as long as he doesn't commit murder...is it any wonder that many elected officials refer to him as *the biggest politician.*

The advantages accruing to bureaucratic officials are because of the positions they hold equip them well to challenge the lawmaker in the area of policy-making. The are specialists in their own problem areas. They come on the scene armed with the *facts,* supported by a personnel staff the size of an army battalion. And they are assured of the permanency of their positions by merit or civil service protection. Is it any wonder the bureaucrat often overshadows the lawmaker? These and other advantages accruing to the bureaucrat because of his position often produce in him a feeling of professional superiority over the elected legislator. The bureaucrat feels that he is *protected, above politics,* and *above other officials.*

When a member of Congress plays the *scratch my back and I will scratch yours* game it can not only increase cost of government, but often projects that are not vital to the general public interest are initiated and expanded. With the majority of the members of the U.S. House of Representatives focusing their efforts on serving constituent needs—*for that's the way to get re-elected* so often cozy rela- tionships take place between the office holder and the bureaucrat. When that association occurs the taxpayers pays the cost.

It has been my experience the bureaucrat is often obsessed with the notion that he must add more and more people to the federal and state employment rolls. In doing so he ignores the need to evaluate the efficiency of his operation. He allows the employee who is no longer productive to stay in his position and creates a second position to duplicate the function of the first. Bureaucratic officials must inject into their departments a substantial interest in evaluating new programs; elimi- nating programs which are no longer needed; reassigning personnel in an efficient and productive manner; and encouraging cooperative efforts between departments. Often, over-zealousness on the part of executive depart- ments to make a name for themselves gets out of hand. Competition between departments and agencies for funds and functions often overshadows the bureaucracy's pri- mary responsibility of serving the public interest.

The lawmaker must be constantly on the alert to spot and expose self-serving bureaucratic claims for increased spending because *the public demands it.* Quite often, the public never demands it. If the public knew about the waste and duplication such spending would bring about, they would be the first to condemn it.

The principle of selecting and promoting employees on the basis of ability and knowledge must always prevail. The rank and file government employee is entitled to equal opportunities, certain job securities, retirement benefits, and proper salaries.

It is administratively unsound for jobs to be put *up for grabs* or placed on the *political block* every time there is an election. No good can come of training a person to do a job only to replace him at the next election with a political appointee, often less qualified, who has to re-learn the same job. With all this the waste, inefficiency, delay, and interruptions are not in the best interest of serving the public. The padding of payrolls *to make room for a certain individual* in turn increases taxes. Government has enough problems related to normal turnover and filling certain skill positions without adding the spoils system to its burden of operation.

However, it might be noted that with the passing of the patronage system, political parties have lost much of their influence, particularly with regard to the recruitment of party workers. Persons who would have attended rallies, helped to get out the vote, assisted with mailings and a thousand other chores because *there's something in it for me* no longer become involved. Their present jobs are secure through civil service.

Government employees, organizations and labor unions become stronger as the number of employees increases. They constitute an influential lobbying force. They are quick to lobby for their own causes. By no means do I condemn anyone for looking out for himself. If persons, engaged in mutual interests, didn't band together to press for their rights, many desirable benefits would probably never materialize. I do, however, feel that government employees should not talk out of *both sides of their mouth* by an appeal for a selfish purpose on one hand and a general *so what attitude* towards elected officials on the other.

After all, government on all levels is the people's business—people who serve it and people who are beneficiaries of the service. The bureaucracy must not be allowed to monopolize the people's business.

The money grab has gotten to the point that more and more states are using taxpayer's money to set up lobbying departments to seek more of the taxpayers' money. States lobbying the federal government for funds has become the *in thing.* With this activity the taxpayer is also paying huge lobbying fees to the District of Columbia based high-priced lobbyist. The National Taxpayers Union has already identified over thirty four million dollars being spent a year regarding state or state agencies lobbying the federal government. Yes, taxpayers dollars are spent to get more taxpayers dollars. Money, Money and more money.

CHAPTER NINE

CONFLICTS OF INTEREST

As we discussed in the previous chapter the potential for conflict of interest can readily occur when significant dollars are contributed to candidates for public office. When a person contributes over a thousand dollars, the least he or she expects is access to the candidate and at the very least to the administrative assistant. However, often the *access comments* are a cover for the real personal or selfish reason for the contribution.

Watergate brought conflict of interest concerns to the surface. In this chapter I am sharing what I witnessed as a state legislator. Most of the points I will bring out can also apply to the Congress. I have watched many honest legislators sweating out a conflict between their duty to the voters and a command from those who supply their daily bread. The outcome of such conflicts helps to explain why government is such a gamble for privilege and monopoly.

A basic dilemma public servants at all levels of government face, but which is especially a conflict for state legislators is: "Which of two master shall I serve?" Because the way state government is structured in our society, the legislator working at this level of public service is caught in a unique and often very difficult position. He owes allegiance to the people who elected him and he has taken an oath to guard the public trust.

Few legislators can financially survive on their legislative salary. Therefore, legislators must also earn a personal livelihood from a private occupation. Sometimes the best interests of his private profession conflict with the best interests of the public. This, of course, is what is referred to in the media and in legal circles as a *conflict of interest*— a situation in which a position of public trust and privilege is capitalized upon to further one's own private gain.

The magnitude of conflict of interest problems on the state level broadens because of the nature of the issues dealt with there. The state lawmaker is right in the thick of societal action. He makes decisions and votes on issues which touch citizens at the grassroots level. He votes on tax measures, school legislation, road and recreational improvements. Yet none of these issues are merely academic to him. Practically every bill which comes before the state legislator will sooner or later have a direct or an indirect effect on him: social, financial or political. He pays taxes; his children go to school in the state; and he drives on state highways to work. It is virtually impossible for him to avoid voting on issues which personally affects him.

The state legislator must also deal with questions and problems which have direct impact upon the profession from which he earns a personal livelihood. For example, he sets policy which affects the real estate business— where highways will be built—interest rates on mortgages, etc. The legislator who deals in real estate in his private life may be faced with a genuine conflict of interest when confronted with legislation regulating the real estate industry. The same is true of the farmer-legislator; banker-legislator; lawyer-legislator. Each may be tempted to serve his private master while neglecting, or down-right abusing his public masters.

No matter what your private profession may be, as a lawmaker, sooner or later some issue is bound to come before the legislative body which will toss that two-sided coin right in front of your face. This is a genuine dilemma lawmakers will face some time in their career. When a conflict is present the legislator should ask to be excused from voting or at the very least disclose the conflict.

This reality, however, should never be a license for the legislator or for any other elected public official, for that matter, to abuse the public trust by blatantly ignoring public interest for private gain. The moral tone of government is a reflection of the moral climate of society at large. If we are to survive as a democracy, our leaders must set an example for the nation and the free world of high moral purpose and selfless action. Unfortunately, this is not always the case. Sadly enough, substantial misuse of public trust for private purposes has been rampant.

I want to emphasize there are many men and women of high integrity, honesty, and sincerity in public office. The dedication, energy, and personal convictions of these people have made our continued survival as a democracy possible. Nevertheless, the number of white-collar subversives, gentlemen conspirators, etc. is sufficiently large to threaten our system of free political institutions. The subversive may be a mayor who embezzles funds; a state offical who accepted a lavish gift; or a federal office holder charged with income tax evasion.

This subversion is not unique. It can be traced back through many generations and administrations on the national, state, and local levels. Truman had the fur coat and deep-freeze scandals; Eisenhower was plagued with the Sherman Adams-Bernard Goldfine incident; the Kennedy years saw the Billie Sol Estes fraud case; Johnson was embarrassed by Bobby Baker; Nixon, Watergate; Carter, the Bert Lance conflict.

In my home state of Maryland, we had our own particular problems with scandal and corruption. The parade of Maryland politicians from the halls of government to the chambers of justice and often on to the Houses of Correction was a sobering spectacle for residents to witness. Former Vice President, Governor of Maryland, and Baltimore County Executive Spiro Agnew of course headed the parade. Others in the entourage included a former U.S. Senator who was convicted of accepting money in return for favorable action on legislation dealing with third class mail rates; Speaker of the House of Delegates was sentenced to three years in prison for mail fraud in the operation of a firm which insured accounts of savings and loan firms; a former Congressman from the eastern shore found guilty of accepting payment for a speech which he gave on the floor of the U.S. House of Representatives; two Baltimore state delegates, who were charged and later convicted of conspiring to conceal a witness in the bribery trial of a Baltimore policeman; a former legislator who was found guilty of accepting a bribe from a County Bowling Proprietors Association to try to amend the law to allow beer to be sold in county bowling alleys; and a Delegate who was also indicted by a federal grand jury on narcotics charges and was gunned down in a Baltimore basement garage and killed before his case came to trial.

We could try to nurse our wounds by trying to rationalize away this haunting spectacle of fallen leaders. We could say politics is no worse than any other profession. Look at television quiz show rackets of some years ago, record business payola price fixing, and conspiracy in large industries, the local bank teller who *misplaces* funds, payoffs to big labor. We could shrug it all off with an attitude that *no matter what you do, it is going to exist.*

But that's self-defeating. More is to be expected of government officials who hold the reigns of power. The public always deserves an honest return on its investment in government. Government officials must not merely reflect the moral tone of the community; they must take an active role in setting a positive example of honesty and integrity. There is no room for rationalizing. Public officials can not be excused from intentional wrongdoing. Inaction and failure to face the problems created by conflict of interest leaves the door open for more and more **graft** and **government payola**.

The whole question of conflict of interest is tied up on so many intricacies, gray areas of moral uncertainty, and matters of good sense that legislators are often left baffled when they seek solutions to the problem. A U.S. Senate Subcommittee reported that, "the problem of ethical standards in government is one which thoughtful men approach with reluctance and humility." And so it is. Few legislators relish playing the part of the white knight reformer who strikes out at practices in the system which have been tacitly approved for years. Few like to accuse his colleagues of wrongdoings. And certainly no one wants to alienate his fellow legislators by giving the impression that he is untainted while everyone else is of questionable character. After all, a legislator's effectiveness in promoting his own proposals is determined to a great extent by his relationships with his colleagues.

The line which separates a genuine conflict of interest situation from one of no conflict is a thin line indeed. Consider the following situations? Do they represent a true conflict of interest, or are they innocent practices?

1. Former legislators and occasionally former state employees appear as lobbyists for special interests immediately after their retirement or defeat from public office. Is this practice legitimate?

2. Prominent party leaders and close personal friends of the chief executive lobby directly for special interests or indirectly through intermediaries who usually are law partners. Do you think this places the governor in direct conflict with the public interest?

3. Law partners of legislators represent private interests. Does this place the lawyer-legislator in conflict when it comes to dividing the office fees received?

4. Legislators engaged in the insurance business increase their business with the state while holding office. Does this obligate the legislator-insurance salesman to support certain measures dealing with insurance?

5. Members of the executive's immediate family or relatives of his close administrative personnel enter in business, such as insurance, bonding, and real estate. All of a sudden, the many persons and firms doing business with the state find it *convenient* to use the services of one of these relatives. Do you think it is ethical?

6. Many prominent appointive positions are awarded as "ego food" in exchange for sizeable party contributions with only face saving concern for the working aspects of the position. Should board or commission members setting the policy for thousands of persons, be appointed on the sole basis of how much money they contributed to a political campaign?

7. Government employees serve as outside consultants to associations or organizations that have an active relationship with the state. Does this place the employee in a position of conflict?

8. State employees moonlight for firms that do business with the state. Can you foresee any possible conflict here?

9. A legislator has a client such as the State Hairdressers Association he represents in the *off legislative season*. The lawmaker then sponsors a bill in their behalf during the legislative session for *services rendered in the legislature* to which he submits an invoice.

10. Paid state commission members who appear before legislature committees are paid lobbyists for special interest groups. Is this proper?

11. Persons who have a large financial stake in their relationship with government are invited to attend an annual *subscription* or *donation* affair in honor of a high official's birthday. Is this a shakedown?

These situations recur time and again, particularly in state legislatures, and often it's difficult to judge whether they represent a conflict of interest.

Certainly, they're not illegal; but that isn't the point. Some people become so obsessed with trying to see how much they can get away with legally, that they lose sight of the public's best interest.

Coping with conflict of interest situations is like engaging in guerrilla warfare in that you never really know who or where the enemy is. A legislator can walk right into a conflict-of-interest ambush without even realizing what is happening to him. I'm not saying that most legislators are innocent bystanders who are dragged into questionable practices against their will or even their knowledge. But in the hands of skilled manipulators, circumstances can be twisted to exert heavy pressure on a legislator to allow the interests of a few to take precedence over the interests of the multitude. Members of Congress can also be put into a vise *if the wrong hands* have in their possession FBI files.

The Congress and most state legislators have passed statutes that deal with fraud and bribery. There are permanent committees within the legislative ranks dealing with ethics. As the profession and business organizations have found out – a code of ethics is essential. The plea for higher standards must be a continual appeal and enforced so as to insure in the best possible way the general public's on-going stake in our democracy. There should be no room for persons in government service, whether elected, appointed, or civil servants, who do not have the broad interest of the public at heart. This interest cannot coexist with selfish and irresponsible personal ambitions. The two just don't mix.

CHAPTER TEN

ABOUT OUR LAWMAKERS

Why do people run for public office? In dealing with this subject the emphasis of this chapter regarding those people running for Congress, state legislation, Mayor, city and county council or commissioner seats. Courthouse related positions such as Clerk of the Court, Tax Collector, Registrar of Wills, Sheriff, etc. reasons for seeking the respective offices can be similar but are more directed to specific career experience. For example, a retired or experienced police officer running for Sheriff and an accountant seeking the County Treasurer's Office. A significant percentage of members of Congress are former state legislators. Mayors and often legislators (state & federal) become governor as former governors often run for the U.S. Senate.

Through the years, however, much less in recent times, political parties would seek out individuals to *fill the ticket*. That is to be certain that candidates for open public office positions are filled. When factions exist within the party *ticket filling* is common place in the primary election. Naturally, when only one candidate files for a given public office there is no primary election and an automatic victory in the General election.

A person who wants to get noticed in political circles generally gets involved in the political process. Many simply get active in a local political party club or become involved with a particular candidate's campaign. Many members of state legislatures and even Congress served in staff positions for members of legislative bodies. The impact of political parties in elections varies from state to state and even within counties in a given state. Few office seekers win unless they have a party label.

More and more the electorate is becoming independent with their vote with voters taking pride in saying *I vote for the person.* As of 1999, forty percent of the national electorate consider themselves as *independent* or *other.* Twenty-seven percent of Americans identify themselves as Republican and thirty-three percent as Democrats. These statistics make it very clear that the *independent voter* determines who is elected our President. Since U.S Senators run state wide similar circumstances occur in their campaigns.

Many times the media place emphasis on the great power of the two major political parties. That power is often overrated. The political party label designation has its greatest impact when it comes to organizing and positioning leadership. With the President, governors, and mayors, limited patronage positions are awarded. The majority winning party of each house of the Congress and state legislatures determines who becomes Speaker, Senate presiding officer, Majority leader and Committee Chairperson. In Maryland, for example, with its large Democratic voter registration I could have never been Majority Leader of the State Senate without being a Democrat. Political parties rarely get involved in legislative issue other than matters related to elections.

There are many reasons why people seek public office. Prestige, power and ego are the most prevalent. To many candidates it is the excitement that goes with winning.

Often candidates surface because the *just don't like* the present office holder of a particular elected office. Run-ins and disagreements with office holders trigger competition. More significant than anything else is the initiative of special causes and interest groups. These lobbying organizations want candidates who agree with their position to become elected to Congress and state legislature. Particularly within the states where legislative election districts are naturally smaller in size than Congressional districts, special interest power can be prevalent. Thus, legislative bodies are made up of what I call *elected lobbyists.* That is single issue focused people who are primarily elected to first serve their parochial interest. That is why legislatures have labor, teacher, trades and professions, etc. representatives and lots of lawyers. Since reapportionment there are fewer lawyers and more and more women and minority members.

Because of numerous *elected lobbyists,* unfortunately, the selfish interest does comes first. This can interfere with what is in the best public interest when it comes to crucial votes. The special interest groups with their money and organized people power carry a real big stick at election time. Single cause group clout can defeat many good lawmakers. A legislator running for re-election knows he may get by and win if one or even two issues advocate groups are against him, but three such pressure organizations on the attack can be a knock-out.

So often very fine and respected citizens who file for public office, and who would probably make good public servants, go down to defeat. This occurs primarily because they didn't properly study the make-up of the electorate, failed to properly look into the record of their opponent, and didn't develop a *winning plan.* So many candidates believe their personal popularity coupled with lots of advertising will bring victory only to find loads of time and money was wasted and their vote accumulation was quite low. First time office seekers who come close to winning can often parlay the defeat into a next time victory. However, in winning elections, as with most everything in life, timing is critically important.

Persons elected to legislative seats, more often than not, feel the importance of their positions. Because they are constantly sought out by voters, asked to give speeches, and are given special courtesies by many they get *wrapped up in the process.* The elected official likes the catered treatment, power, and prestige. More often than not his or her focus is on *how long can I stay here.* With this being a permanent focus numerous legislative decisions are made with the next election constantly *on the mind.*

Although many lawmakers are already committed to special interests prior to their election, this in itself is not all bad. Often they can share valuable information. The unfortunate aspect is sometimes their special cause focus receives priority over many other important matters.

After much thought and analysis, this writer feels the typical legislative body is made up as follows:

Legislative Designation	Percentage of Members
Issue Advocate Lawmakers	60%
Somewhat Independent Lawmakers	25%
Mavericks	10%
"Over the Edge" Members	5%

Many legislators become so embedded in the systems that their power increases with each passing election.

Seniority significance means many lawmakers who seek leadership positions have to *wait their turn,* thus the need to make many decisions and to keep *running* in order to achieve their goal. Recalling my four terms it went like this: first term exciting and *getting my feet wet*; second term confidence in myself and the decisions I was making made me *quite comfortable*; third term as I advanced in leadership things were somewhat *boring and repetitive*; fourth term *felt more effective* only because of being in a leadership role. However, it was indeed a most exhausting experience. During this sixteen year period I looked for openings hopefully to be positioned to run for the U.S. Senate. Such never occurred and running for the U.S. House of Representative was an option I passed up twice. I didn't like the two year term—the raising of money—and waiting forever to move up the ladder.

Large percentages of lawmakers are very comfortable in their positions and stay as long as they can often winning re-election without opposition and remaining in legislative bodies for decades. In state legislature, in particular, they can become statesmen who are genuine public watch dogs. They are able to spot the *legislative snakes* (bad parts of legislative bills) and are able to *kill bad legislation* that otherwise would probably pass without their presence. They have no desire to advance up the political ladder. This is good and it can be bad. If the elected official solely focuses on his or her popularity and providing constituent services—and doesn't deal with major legislative concerns—such is not in the broad best interest of the public. I have always been quite cognizant of this, for the person I defeated in my first primary for the State Senate, was a sixteen year House veteran who in all those years never sponsored a major piece of legislation. That fact became the issue that permitted me to chalk up a victory.

It is Congress that should receive the closest scrutiny by the electorate. Each election, out of the 435 members of the House of Representatives, only about twenty percent are *up for grabs*. That means eighty percent of the members are in safe seats and will get re-elected and some without opposition. Naturally, House seats open up when House members run for six year term U.S. Senate positions. Why does this happen? Each member of Congress with his or her own consistency is a *big-shot*. With this role and high honor they have a staff in Washington, D.C. and offices within their congressional district in the respective states. Tremendous focus on constituent services, and wide use of perks available to them, they can constantly enhance and perpetuate their personal position. They use the media to the fullest extent with staff members focused on media opportunities and putting on the best spin. Taping occurs directly from the Capitol and *is fed* to the media *back home*. This is being done with taxpayer dollars. Members of Congress have their own agendas, which makes it most difficult for Congressional leaders to expeditiously respond to many national issues.

Until such time as there is Congressional Term limitation, concentration on getting re-elected will always be the higher priority. Congress is just loaded with sub-committees and more sub-committees so members can have chairmanships and look that much more important. These committees require staffs and facilities. Numerous committees and sub-committees are dealing with the same issue. I feel terms of members of the U.S. House of Representatives should be four years instead of two years, with a limit of three terms, not to exceed twelve years. U.S. Senate terms remain at six years with a limit of two terms thus, a person first elected to the House and then the Senate could serve as long as twenty-four years.

In this media age, members of Congress need to project the proper image. Therefore, considerable time is spent on *communicating with the voters* with the full use of the electronic media and massive mailings to constituents paid for by you, the taxpayer. It's like an on going political campaign at the public's expense. As with state legislatures, members of Congress live with the seniority system. Breaks do come when one political party gets control of a given House and thus majority leadership roles change.

It is not the intent to condemn good and effective constituent services. The concern is there is not enough attention given to dealing expeditiously when it comes to most national matters. Members of Congress, even with what is seen by many as receiving too high salaries, do have the need to have two bases of operation, that is, one in the state and one in Washington D.C. Unlike many state legislatures, being a member of Congress is a full time position.

What becomes somewhat frightening is numerous Congressional members get so caught up in the *web of their own importance* an attitude of *as long as I keep my base covered back home I'll be okay.* The Washington scene really becomes their true home. With lobbying, bureaucratic mingling and inter-play, the federal government keeps growing, and dollar expenditures keep piling up on top of billions and more billions of dollars. In all legislative halls, not enough time is given to oversight and closing down empires that are no longer needed.

Fortunately for all of us—although it is a rarity, but it does happen—there are a few leaders who will take an unpopular position on a given issue. In doing so they perform a great public service and put aside their own self-interest. Dynamic and effective leaders should spend their energies convincing American citizens why their position is the right way to go. Here is where some masterful bold-type **spinning** could be put to real good use.

CHAPTER ELEVEN

THE INFLUENCE PEDDLERS

No realistic representation of government would be complete without the familiar figures who frequent the halls, committee rooms, and offices of the Congress and legislatures to try to win favor for their organizations or causes. These are the lobbyists—the influence peddlers—who seek to catch a legislator's ear, explain their organization's position to him, win his or her vote.

They espouse many causes, represent many groups, operate under many different titles or names. I classify them as follows:

The Legislative Representative. This person is a professional employee of a commercial business, trade association, or professional society that has a large financial stake in what happens during legislative sessions. He usually bears the title of _Executive Director, Director of Public Relations, Manager_ or _Executive Secretary._ As a full-time employee he generally becomes adept in the art and science of influencing legislators. Also in this classification are representatives of labor unions, railroad brotherhoods, and similar organizations who, although elected by the membership, derive their primary income from the organization they represent.

Special Assignment Representative. This person is usually a lawyer, a former legislator, or an official of a private enterprise who is hired by an organization and paid an attractive fee to represent that group's interests in particular legislation. He may be a well-known public figure, top bracket lawyer, little known attorney, or local citizen. Generally, he is not solely dependent upon lobbying activities for his income.

Volunteer Representative. This person receives no compensation, often not even expenses, for his or her efforts in behalf of an active pressure group. He usually carries the title of chairman of the group's legislative committee and could be from the League of Women Voters, the Parent Teacher Association, or the Society for the Prevention of Cruelty to Animals. Many of the volunteer representatives serve in their legislative positions for a short time, while others become permanent fixtures in legislative corridors. As government has grown larger and more complex, the numbers, strength, and monetary commitment attached to the lobbying profession have grown to such proportions that it is often referred to as *The Third House of the Legislature.* As discussed in Chapter One I prefer to refer to it as an *Influence Branch.*

The average citizen seems to look upon the lobbyist with even more distrust and skepticism than he does the elected official. If the public hears the lobbyist and legislator are working closely together, immediately wrong doing is inferred and the worst is expected. Every state house in the nation has been suspected or openly accused, at one time or another, of being little more than a marketplace for fancy wheeling and dealing, big money payoffs, and the most sordid acts of corruption imaginable. But sometimes the cynicism regarding the corruptibility of legislators emanates from the lawmakers themselves.

Despite its unsavory connotations, lobbying has a sound legal and practical base. Legally, the first amendment to the United States Constitution grants to the people the unhindered right to petition the government for a redress of grievances. Practically, the lobbyists can provide a valuable and needed service for the modern day legislator.

Like it or not, lobbying will probably exist as long as we have a democratic elective form of government. Show me a single legislative session without the appearance of lobbyists, and I'll show you a greatly handicapped legislative body. The tremendous acceleration of issues before legislatures—many of which are technical and complex, coupled with the scarcity of information available to the legislator—create a vital need for specialized and general citizen input to the legislative process in the form of advice.

However, along with the need for lobbying as a service to the Congress and the legislatures, comes an equally strong need for control. For amid the shouts of the organized and vocal lobbyists, the unorganized and forgotten majority, (the public), often goes unheard in the legislative process. Therefore, the public deserves proper control of lobbying activities so that the general interest is protected.

Although most states have adopted some type of lobbying legislation, it is limited in most cases to statutes dealing with the public disclosure of lobbying activities. The states that do have lobbying control laws have usually enacted them only after blatant abuses and scandals have forced public demand for correction.

Beyond codes of ethics dealing with outright fraud, there has been little general interest among lobbyists themselves to raise their professional standards. It seems absurd to me that a lobbying group engaged professionally in a form of public relations would permit an unethical minority in its ranks to corrupt its public image. The lobbying interests owe it to themselves to *get their house in order* nearly as much as they owe it to the public to correct the abuses of their profession.

Every legislator gets to know many lobbyists intimately—the more intimately, the better, as far as the lobbyist is concerned. A legislator, regardless how hard he may try, can not avoid contact with lobbyists. Both parties must follow the unspoken *ground rules* of diplomacy toward each other if their relationship is to be a mutually *livable* one. The legislator needs to treat the lobbyist with courtesy when the latter comes to present his story on a legitimate mission. However, on the lobbyist's part, the uncontrolled *anything goes* approach is taboo and must be checked with self-imposed standards and self-discipline.

Any ethical and seasoned lobbyist knows his first step toward success is the ability to recognize, understand, and respect the positions of those who oppose him. And, if he plans to be successful, he has to remember *there will be another time.* The surest way for the lobbyist to *burn out* and be forced to *pick up his marbles and go home* is to lose his temper, threaten, or apply nasty pressure to conscientious lawmakers. The lobbyist who wants to win the respect of the legislator and influence his vote must first conduct himself in a well-principled manner and have a sound understanding of the issue in which he is interested. As with any kind of selling, there are two key factors: the impression made by the salesperson and the appeal of the product. There is no question that in securing the support of legislators, both of these factors influence the results. To the legislator, the lobbyist can be a good friend or an ardent enemy. The lobbyist, by his own actions, can often harm the position of those he represents, even generating legislative resistance where it did not previously exist. When the lobbyist gives the **spin** as to his viewpoint it must be accurate. A lobbyist who has enjoyed a good reputation for many years can destroy it by switching to hard pressure tactics, receiving exorbitant fees for services, becoming over-confident in his approach or *asking for too much*, legislatively speaking.

Let's take a closer look at each of the three categories of lobbyists, with attention given to possible reform of ethical standards in each classification:

LEGISLATIVE REPRENTATIVE

The professional *Legislative Representative* is usually very well versed in the workings of the legislative process. He knows his own job might be dependent upon how his legislative *score card* is tallied by his organization. He further knows that each appearance before Congress and legislatures will not be his last one; he does not want to overplay his hand. He knows the risks of overexposure. Many legislative representatives will go through an entire legislative session without ever finding it necessary to make a stand on a single issue. Often there will be issues of only minor importance to them, so they will *take their chances on the outcome* and say very little.

A legislator will see these lobbyists as often as he sees his own legislative colleagues. For the legislative representatives, the halls of Congress and State Houses are headquarters. Their briefcases serve as desks; their offices are wherever they can find a spot in the corridors. They report to work each day along with the legislator and leave when the last bell for the day rings.

Each day they attempt to accomplish their mission by making contacts to present their viewpoints to the legislators. This usually occurs between committee hearings, telephoning, or office visits. As they become interested in specific legislation they have difficulty trying not to look too obvious or eager to some lawmakers while trying to catch up with others. As they bounce about and try to stage a performance, a complete switch in a legislator's plans can immediately crush a lobbyist's expectations. There are long periods of waiting and anticipating. These lobbyists must be constantly *sure* of where they stand by taking a straw vote of what support they have, don't have, or might get. They have to try to make sure that their legislative supporters don't leave them; they must remind other lawmakers to remember *to talk for* the particular bill in committee; at the very least, they must try to make sure their bill doesn't get lost in the shuffle.

In my opinion, the biggest enemy of the *Legislative Representative* is over-exposure. It is often difficult for a successful lobbyist to ease up a little, send down an assistant, or *sit out* a legislative session now and then; but for the good of the organization he represents, his *absence from felicity* almost becomes a must if he is to retain a good batting average year after year. Most legislative representatives are extremely courteous and tactful. As a group these lobbyist are generally smart enough to know that protocol and finesse are required in the successful and acceptable performance of their responsibilities.

Seldom does the legislative representative capture the public limelight. But for him, there is strength in anonymity. He is scrupulous in his testimony before the committee hearings, particularly if the news media representatives are present, for under no circumstances does he ever want to be misquoted. His principal interest is the organization he represents and, as its agent, the prudent legislative representative only wants to be a *big man* with its members. However, mass organizations such as labor unions and teachers associations are exceptions to this rule. It is often their legislative representative's advantage to be well known.

The legislative representative probably knows more about individual legislators than legislators know about each other. It is important for him to know their economic backgrounds, political ties, and legislative interests. He reports to the membership, usually via a house publication, on how the various legislators voted on the issues which interest the organization. Although all voting records are a matter of public concern, the lobbyists treads on explosive ground if he overly emphasizes those who voted against his position. This legislative representative may have little future chance to win over the *victimized* legislator. Instead of being negative in his reporting, the wise legislative representative will praise those who supported his position and simply not mention the others.

Of the three types discussed, the Legislative Representative is the group with the most serious claim to professional status. Their lobbying work is a full-time commitment. Since lobbying produces their major source of income, they become a *permanent attachment* to Congress and the legislature's. They are the leadership group within the lobbyist fraternity.

This category of lobbyists counts many lawyers among its ranks. These are part-time lobbyists—often prominent political figures, former members of Congress and the legislatures, friends of the executive branch or top-notch legal experts who capitalize on their acquaintances, *inside* knowledge and expertise to influence legislators for their special interests. Seldom do any of these lobbyists come *cheap* to the interest they represent. When newspaper accounts reveal sensational lobbying fees, the general public becomes bewildered and frustrated. They wonder if the legislator who makes a smaller salary might have shared in his high income.

Most cases of unethical legislative representation, as well as outright corruption and fraud, have occurred among part-time or occasional lobbyists. There are entirely too many who are obviously interested in large fees. Most legislators are inclined to become suspicious of them. Many special assignment lobbyists are there to *cash in* on campaign promises which are most always associated with contributions; they are there for *their share*; or because *it is due us*. With money the target, there is little concern for ethics. This kind of lobbying definitely harms the public image of both the politician and the lobbyist.

VOLUNTEER REPRESENTATIVES

The volunteer lobbyist, who is usually a member of a well organized pressure group, is perfectly harmless and often persuasive. He is enthusiastic about his mission. However, because he has been well indoctrinated in what his group wants, he usually doesn't like to settle for less than the whole pie. Seldom is he willing to accept the reality that there are other groups placing tremendous demands and pressures on the Congress and Legislatures.

There is no question that his influence is substantial for he is from *back home* and often a friend or supporter of the legislator. In any event, the lawmaker doesn't welcome the prospect of having him as a political enemy. He is usually present to ask for more financial aid for a specific cause. He often intimidates a conscientious legislator, even though it is obvious that he sometimes doesn't really know enough of the facts. A legislator doesn't question his integrity, for it is obvious that he is acting in good faith. When he comes to the Capitol, he might lose a day or so of pay from work and he often has the personal expense of travel and meals.

Usually the volunteer representative will work closely with a professional lobbyist who has a shared interest. His visits to Congress and legislatures are staged at a critical voting time so he can sit up in the gallery with his tally sheet and mark in the *yeas* and *nays* as he looks down on the law-makers. The vote for which he is present is usually a *test vote*; as the bill comes out of committee, it is placed on the calendar for second reading, and still must come up again for third reading and final passage. If a legislator voted against the lobbying representative's position—and more votes for his side are still needed—the elected representatives can expect an avalanche of telegrams in the morning, telephone calls, and excessive corridor *button holing*.

The dedicated volunteer, once he learns to temper his passion and zeal for his cause with ample knowledge of the legislative process—and skillful preparation and presentation of his facts—can be astonishingly effective. Even the most dissident lawmaker can appreciate the amateur lobbyist adversary who has the ability to remain cool and intelligently respond to the sharpest questions a hostile committee member can fire.

There is no question that the heated demands of pressure groups represent the wishes of only a minority of our population and that, through their own initiative and leadership, they have been able to have the *organized say* over the *unorganized silent*. The impact of this minority pressure may be measured in different ways. Their **spin machine** works overtime in bringing about influence. There can be little question that they have been extremely successful, particularly, if success is to be measured by the number of legislative proposals that have passed or died with their sanction.

Any discussion of **spin techniques** would not be complete without at least identifying the different lobbyists. **Influence Peddlers** have a tremendous impact as to what takes place in legislative circles. The impact can have lasting effects.

CHAPTER TWELEVE

CALL 'EM AS YOU SEE 'EM

There is a certain awe that overcomes every new lawmaker who is anxious to perform his or her duties responsibly. I've seen the symptoms appear even in those with the highest credentials for intellectual capacity and political wisdom. It occurs on that first vote you cast after you've taken the oath of office. At that moment, the importance of the office has its full impact on those who take legislative responsibility seriously. Remarkably opinionated and decisive men have been humbled at this moment which one must experience to fully appreciate.

I'll never forget my first roll call vote as a state legislator. The Senate Committee on Judicial Proceedings, on which I was serving, was considering an extremely controversial piece of legislation—just the sort of bill to put any legislator, especially a new one on the spot. I could see merits to both sides of the question and I realized that I would have to make a decision. The hearing had just ended when the chairman called for a roll call vote. When my name was read, being extra cautious to do the right thing, particularly on my first vote as a legislator, I paused a second or so to nervously clear my throat. Just at that point, the veteran Chairman said, *George, just call 'em as you see 'em.*

After the experience of four legislative terms, I sure know what the committee chairman meant. Making decisions is a legislator's primary role. He must be able to size up a problem or a situation, review as many angles of it as possible, and then reach a decision on his own which he feels will be in the best public interest. Ideally a legislator is supposed to vote independently and impartially. He is supposed to be able to withstand and properly evaluate pressures from those who try to influence his vote. He is supposed to *call 'em as he sees 'em.* But can he always, and does he always?

The legislator who tries to *call 'em as he sees 'em* must struggle with pressure from many sources around him who want him to call things the way others see them. Just as the electorate is influenced by certain elements to cast its vote for a particular candidate, the legislator also takes certain factors into account when he makes his decisions on the problems which come before him.

The factors that determine the voters' choice are many and complex: his economic status; ancestral voting habits; intellectual capacity; party ties; first impression of the candidates; persuasion; perceptions; prejudices; hatreds, etc. It sometimes seems that only a small percentage of voters cast their ballots according to the issues. Add to all this the **spin** the opposing advocates give to the specific piece of legislation, and one will witness heavy pressure.

Many of the same influences which guide the electorate toward its vote also work on the legislator as he makes his decision on individual pieces of legislation. As I see it, there are seven major factors that determine how a legislator will vote. We have already devoted attention to four of these influences—lobbying, bureaucracy, campaign contributions and the power of the news media. I will just briefly mention them with the other three factors receiving more description.

The seven factors which influence the legislator, and consequently play an important part in shaping the fate of proposed legislation are:
- Executive Department Impact
- Lobbyist, Pressure Groups, Political Parties
- Bureaucracy Influence
- Campaign Contributions
- Power of the News Media
- Influence of Colleagues
- Public Opinion, Compromising and Personal Convictions

EXECUTIVE DEPARTMENT IMPACT

The influence of the President, governor, mayor and other administrative officials on a legislator's vote varies according to the strength of certain key elements: the constitutional powers of the executive; the political affiliation of the executive in comparison to the legislative majority; the individual personality and leadership characteristics of the executive and the susceptibility of legislative personalities to *incentive* enticements—executive rewards distributed to team members who play along with the game plan.

It's hardly surprising that many legislators at one time or another in their career succumb to the incentive enticement syndrome. Most politicians want to improve their positions and no one can quarrel with aggressiveness and a drive to get ahead. Some legislators may seek to increase their power and prestige within the Congress and the legislatures by attempting to secure leadership positions. They also may seek higher political office. Other lawmakers set their sights on appointive offices—a judgeship, the head position of a department, agency, etc. These offices may bring higher salaries, greater prestige, and perhaps a welcome relief from the hectic pace in serving as a legislator.

The frustrations and pressures that accompany political competition are enough to make any elected official start to think about other more secure and less demanding areas. Often, a state legislator is expected to be *all things to all people*. My description of a legislator responding to his constituents goes something like this:

> *His or her personal business office or home becomes a public information center, clearing house, branch office of the nearest employment agency, letter writing—secretarial service, scholarship advice headquarters, notary public endorsement bureau, complaint department, place to go to cut the "red tape," a ward healer's paradise, influence center, political theory institute and last (and usually least) a place to discuss legislation or, more usually, to oppose it. These functions the legislator tries to perform with a small staff as an avalanche of telephone calls are trying to be returned, business and family commitments are met in between banquets, meetings, dedications and hearings.*

Is it any wonder that the legislator may become overwhelmed with his responsibility and begin to think how pleasant it would be to step away from the turmoil and grasp a nice juicy political plum?

For the legislator who wants higher office; for the official who eyes lucrative appointive positions; and even for the passive representative who only wants to retain his seat, as if he were participating in an endurance contest to *sit* there and *just get by*: these career ambitions can often be satisfied by a simple executive flick of the finger.

But in return for the legislator getting what he wants—or at least a likely assurance that he will eventually get what he wants—the legislator pays a price. And the price is high. He is no longer totally independent in his voting choices. In political terminology, he has *sold out*. He has become a team member and the influence of the executive has risen to primary importance among the many factors which will determine how he votes on any particular issue. *I'll just have to give the Governor this one*, he figures. His number one consideration in voting on issues before the legislature must now be not to *upset* the President or the Governor.

Elected officials want to be the big man back home, and often a kind word from the Executive can make him stand taller in the eyes of his constituents. The executive's influence may determine the outcome of that *special project* every legislator at some point desires. Such can make it easier for the legislator to *play ball*. However, the lawmakers must also be wary of falling prey to executive enticements. They can clearly threaten his independence and make the influence of the executive the supreme factor in determining how he or she votes.

LOBBYISTS, PRESSURE GROUPS, AND POLITICAL PARTIES

As we discussed, the lobbyist finds his greatest strength in influencing the legislators is to be forthright and honest. The legislator knows that he has to pay attention to powerful interests. Political parties have always occupied a central position in our American system of government. The strength of the political party depends upon how intense the competition is for control of the legislative lobby.--

BUREAUCRACY INFLUENCE

The influence of the bureaucrat on the individual lawmaker's vote depends very much on the public relations abilities of the departments and agencies and how these skills are perceived by individual legislators. It is just as easy for a legislator to strongly support a department's program as it is for his colleague to bitterly oppose it. Bureaucrats can become **master spinners** in their own right. Personal experiences with a department, impressions, and other human elements play a primary role in determining lawmakers attitudes towards bureaucrats.

CAMPAIGN CONTRIBUTIONS

Campaign contributions absolutely influence a legislator's vote. A careful review of contributions to a legislator and his later support of special interest legislation emphasizes the impact. As we have discussed money power has great influence.

POWER OF THE NEWS MEDIA

This influence is felt as keenly by the legislator at the state and local level as it is at the national level. Every legislator knows that he is subjected to constant public review through the eyes of reporters and commentators who sit at the press table. Every legislator also knows how much public reactions and opinions mean to his present success as a legislator and to any future political ambitions he may have. No politician wants bad press. In an effort to look favorable in the public light, many legislators will go out of their way to support measures that will *make news* or generate good editorial opinions. The influence of the press in shaping the legislator's vote derives much of its strength from the dependency, of the public and elected official alike, on the media. The legislator interacts with a battery of reporters at work in the legislative halls. The relationship between elected officials and the press may be one of mutual respect or one of mutual fear.

COLLEAGUES' INFLUENCE

In discussing the factors which shape the decision of the lawmaker as he votes on public policy matters, the spotlight is most often placed on the President or the Governor. However, sometimes and so often not even realized, the real motivating factor behind the legislator's decision may be the influence of the legislative *fraternity.*

It has often been said that the legislative process is nothing more than *formalized horse trading.* This characterization is somewhat brutal. As with any group or organization, the mutual interests, responsibilities and sense of belonging of its members create a tie that becomes a part of every member of the Congress and legislatures. This is so often a *legislative courtesy* custom. What this means is that under normal circumstances, legislators assume that each representative knows best what legislation should be enacted for his or her own district or state. Therefore, the supremacy of each legislator in affairs of his or her own district is a matter of legislative courtesy.

Personal pleas from one legislator to another of *I need one more vote* carry substantial influence in determining the fate of certain pieces of legislation. A bill may have no strong meaning to some lawmakers one way or another, but to the sponsor it is extremely important. The chances are the sponsor will get the votes he needs as long as he makes his position known, for every legislator knows that sometime or another he might need an additional vote. When all is said and done, after the executive, the lobbyists and the press is quieted, it is the fellow legislator who gets to make the last plea for influence. He is physically in your midst; he can send a note across the room or whisper to a fellow member. A form of lobbying, one might say, but still an elected official carrying out the responsibilities of his office.

PUBLIC OPINION, COMPROMISING, AND PERSONAL CONVICTIONS

One of the most difficult tasks for anyone, and the public official is no exception, is to determine public opinion. It can assume many guises. It can be correct today, of little or no value tomorrow. It can be manipulated and spun to suit many purposes, some good and others bad. Public opinion is most influenced by radio, television and newspaper. What passes for "public opinion" may only be the voice of a small minority sounding like the majority; it may be the brainchild of a clever advertising or public relations man that knows how to spin things; it may be a creation of an opposing faction full of hate; it may take the form of an expression about an individual or event.

With our elections becoming more and more like business sales campaigns—with all-out promotions, creation of *images*, with *buyer appeal*—public opinion can be shaped by a few experts. As we discussed the role of the professional pollster has grown with increased use of the mass media in political campaigns. Even though the *polling experts* have been known to be wrong they continue to be listened to. Sometimes they appear to influence the very things they are polling. The polls become the **media spin**. The lawmakers, due to the fact that he represents a limited district, is generally in a better position than most national legislators to take the *pulse*.

Public opinion is not a single phenomenon. It is multiple. There are many public opinions and the successful politician must be sensitive to them. Human brains form opinions. Daily work, attendance in schools, fraternal and social affiliations, church participation, prejudices, etc., mold basic ideals. The sensitive areas beyond the basic functions are most critical for the politician. So often the opinion with the broadest base lies hidden within the rank and file of the unorganized majority. No matter how much a legislator may try to escape reality and claim that his *position* is the absolute and only solution, it doesn't take long for him to realize that the very nature of the legislative process requires compromise. The offering of amendments to legislation in itself is compromising. When each of us takes a close look at our personal lives, we will also find a continuous series of compromises.

The real question should be, *does the compromise totally change the purpose of the legislation or water it down to the point where no legislation would be better?* Lobbyists, pressure groups and bureaucrats are constantly saying to the legislators, *we find the purpose of the bill to be good and will support its passage, as long as we are exempt.* Everyone trying to protect his own narrow interest has led to many bills being declared unconstitutional, courts legislating instead of interpreting, and some statutes of little or no value cluttering law books. This kind of pressure, along with a fair share of normal mistakes, causes a lot of peculiar things to happen, especially when the sponsor of the bill adamantly fights for its passage because *he needs the bill.*

Much good legislation has come out of compromising. On many occasions, if more sensible and cooperative compromising were achieved, there might have been less extreme class legislation. Compromising in itself can bring opposing forces together and build mutual understanding. There is no question that the legislator's political burden can be lightened through legislative compromise. However, when compromising is in direct conflict with individual principles and conscience, it has no place in the legislative halls or elsewhere.

Some legislators feel that too much statesmanship and independent thinking are a good way to stir up opposition and not get re-elected. But is it fair to measure public service by how long you can serve in one job?

Some legislators, unfortunately, find that the easiest way to get elected and re-elected, time in and time out, is to do just enough to get by. Instead of ambitiously facing the challenge of the office, this type of lawmaker engages in a public relations campaign based on the theory that *if I don't act, no one can complain.* Time catches up with some; others, because of public concern *for that nice man;* or through enough memories of *the letter I received from him some years ago,* get re-elected. Every legislative body has its share of such personalities. The political ambitions do not go beyond what they are now doing. With responsibility so great—numerous problems to be solved—much service to be rendered—there is no room for inaction or the necessity to say to a legislator, *Don't just sit there, do something!*

Every lawmaker is confronted with the dilemma of, *do I vote the way the people I represent want me to, or do I vote the way I personally feel is proper?* Needless to say, this is a most difficult question and one that has long perplexed thoughtful men. In the first place, unless the legislator is a master magician, he will have a difficult time in defining *what the people want.* Here is where the public opinion may not be what the pressure groups, influence peddlers, and **spinmeisters** dictate.

I often wonder how much more effective certain able legislators might have been if they could always vote on issues without having to think about the next election. Legislators who become obsessed with future political dreams and aspirations are likely to have foremost in their minds, *what political value does this have for me?* From a practical standpoint, there is little room for quarreling with that question; but, at the same time, *every man must live with himself* and although the *outside* consequences may be hard to live with, a decision from within as to *what is right,* and *what my conscience dictates* must be the final word.

When the voters elect a person to public office they hand over the responsibilities of representation to him or her. In the legislative process, it is up to the individual judgment of each member to determine what is in the best interest of the constituents he represents.

Every legislator sees genuine acts of dedication, principle, and belief. Many individual stands on issues require courage and stamina: a vote against an issue that a close friend wanted you to support; a vote opposite that of a strong pressure block; voting for a measure when a heavy campaign against it made it look like anyone supporting it was under contract to a lobbyist; making a strong stand against the position of a person you like and respect, but with whom you completely disagree.

Most lawmakers could write a doctoral thesis on their individual voting experiences. With all the pressure and other factors which will determine how a legislator will vote, it is often just amazing how good the result can be. Our democratic system of government has survived because many lawmakers have had the courage to withstand many pressures and really *call 'em as they see 'em.*

CHAPTER THIRTEEN

YOU HAVE MORE POWER THAN YOU REALIZE

The question is not will I have politics, but, what kind. As we enter the 21st Century and reflect on the American experiment in democracy, which is just over two-hundred and twenty-four years old, there is so much our great country has achieved. The vision of our founding fathers has been remarkable as they conceived a government of the people, by the people and for the people. Our history and civics books have extolled the praises and virtues of American democracy. We, as citizens, can look back with pride upon a heritage of many heroic deeds, high principles, and dedicated people. Other nations throughout the world have found that our open elections really work.

Far too many Americans, around half of the two hundred and five million Americans eligible to vote, sit on the sideline and don't even exercise their vote. Thus, a majority of the population is not participating. So often we hear citizens shrug off the responsibility of voting with comments like: *If I vote, it will just cancel out my wife's vote; It doesn't matter whether I vote or not—one side is just as bad as the other; or There's no use in voting—you can't buck the system; That's the way it is* attitudes are not acceptable. In my experience as a legislator, I have seen bills before the State Senate, which affect the lives of millions of people, either rise to victory or fall to defeat because of one legislator's vote. Just one vote granted statehood to California, Idaho, Oregon, Texas and Washington. The Draft Act of World War II was passed by one vote in the U.S. House of Representatives.

Thomas Jefferson in 1880 and John Quincy Adams in 1825 were each elected to the Presidency by one vote in the electoral college. The most famous illustration of the power of a single vote came when Rutherford B. Hayes' election as President was contested and referred to an electoral commission. He emerged the victor by one vote. The man who cast that deciding vote was a Congressman from Indiana, a lawyer who was also elected to Congress by a margin of just one vote—a vote cast by one of his clients who, though desperately ill, insisted on being taken to the polls to vote!

Just look, for a moment, at some examples of individual and collective citizen action which has had an effect on government. Ralph Nader, for instance, the highly publicized champion of the consumer, whatever you may think of his crusade, has made a difference. Yet, in the early stages of his endeavor, he was just one voice in the crowd—just an average citizen who probably asked himself the same question; *What can one man do?* Common Cause, the organization which operates from Washington, D.C. has pressed for extensive reform. It grew from a modest organization of average citizens into an influential national organ which functions as combined public accountant and citizens' lobby. The National Taxpayers Union that started with one person, James Dale Davidson, over thirty years ago has kept track of fiscal voting records of Members of Congress. This organization has become so strong that it has been able to challenge the federal government on many occasions in and out of the courts.

Do take another look, at your personal single largest dollar investment, which is for the cost of government. Think about how important participating in our democracy is to you and your family. Are you feed up and feel you *have been had?* Then take a look at some of the people holding public office and do your personal evaluation of them. Learn to know the ones to whom you feel you can relate. Get active in a candidate's political campaign. You may feel it is so distant but it is reachable and they welcome the assistance. If you prefer, jump in and attend a meeting of the political party or club of your choice. See beyond the **spin** and find out what is going on for yourself. Our political system is crying out for fresh ideas, zeal and the infusion of new energy and dedication to the responsibilities of elective representation. Watch carefully the elected official who is bragging about *bringing home the bacon* as you get a handle on the *larger perspective.*

Consider organizing a town meeting. In doing so you do not feel you are going it alone. A friend of mine who was Chairperson for the legislative committee of a Sanford, Florida organization held town meetings all the way from Governor down to the school board. The meetings always attracted much media attention and were well attended.

We also fervently need the young to prevent our democratic system from stagnating. To attract young people into politics, we must all seek to inject some basic respect for the profession back into the hearts and minds of the people. After all the ancient Greeks taught that politics is the most honorable and useful of all the professions. They referred to it as the *art of statesmanship.* Remember, Washington, Franklin, Jefferson and Lincoln were politicians.

Good politics brings about good government. Our democratic form of government was not nurtured from despair but from positive response.

At the very least, consider joining the P.A.I. That is the *Public Awareness Institute* of which you are the President and Chief Executive Officer. Whether you are the single member, or your family and friends become a part of the institute, you can do considerable good by just being *aware.* You don't have to be a sitting duck. You don't need to be **conned**. You do have the obligation to *see through* what is being **spun** your way.

ACKNOWLEDGMENT

The writing of this book was only possible since the voters of Maryland gave me the privilege of serving sixteen years in the State Senate. My involvement as President of the National Taxpayer's Union and National Chairman of the Committee for a Constitutional Amendment for a Balanced Budget permitted me to testify before forty legislative committees. Making a short run for Governor of Maryland and withdrawing six weeks later, with recognition that the *money in the system* made a victory at the time nearly impossible, was an encounter never to be forgotten. Also, the experience of taking a long shot attempt to win a U.S. Senate seat from Florida gave me a further opportunity to inter-face and learn more about the media. To all involved, many thanks.

I particularly want to express gratitude to my wife Karen for all she does and for putting up with me. To my son, Chip, a lawyer and co-author of the book, *Your PQ Is Showing-Perception is Powerful,* and step-son, Todd Templin, a television executive producer, my appreciation to both for your able feed-back. To my senior cousin (through marriage), Randy Mason for superb editing, son-in-law John Ovitz for his structure ideas, Carl Schilke for the sub-title suggestions, and Penny Wolford for ably typing the manuscript, I express my sincere gratitude.

Thank You